T0375593

PRIME
for the
PUMP

A unique collection of stories and sermons to warm the hearts and inspire the minds of preachers, teachers, and believers of every age and from all walks of life.

PHILIP W. McLARTY

WESTBOW
PRESS®
A DIVISION OF THOMAS NELSON
& ZONDERVAN

WestBow Press books may be ordered through booksellers or by contacting:

WestBow Press
A Division of Thomas Nelson & Zondervan
1663 Liberty Drive
Bloomington, IN 47403
www.westbowpress.com
844-714-3454

Because of the dynamic nature of the Internet, any web addresses or links contained in this book may have changed since publication and may no longer be valid. The views expressed in this work are solely those of the author and do not necessarily reflect the views of the publisher, and the publisher hereby disclaims any responsibility for them.

Any people depicted in stock imagery provided by Getty Images are models, and such images are being used for illustrative purposes only. Certain stock imagery © Getty Images.

Scripture quotations marked (NIV) are taken from the Holy Bible, New International Version®, NIV®. Copyright ©1973, 1978, 1984, 2011 by Biblica, Inc.™ Used by permission of Zondervan. All rights reserved worldwide. www. zondervan.comThe "NIV" and "New International Version" are trademarks registered in the United States Patent and Trademark Office by Biblica, Inc.™

Scripture quotations marked (RSV) are taken from Revised Standard Version of the Bible, copyright © 1946, 1952, and 1971 National Council of the Churches of Christ in the United States of America. Used by permission. All rights reserved worldwide.

Interior Image Credit: Rodney Steele (photo of author)

ISBN: 979-8-3850-4523-5 (sc)
ISBN: 979-8-3850-4522-8 (e)

Library of Congress Control Number: 2025904339

Print information available on the last page.

WestBow Press rev. date: 04/01/2025

Contents

Dedication

This book is dedicated to preachers, teachers, seminary students, saints, and seekers, who labor week after week parsing the scriptures looking for inspiration to give voice to the Word of God, yet who, at times, need prime for the pump to whet their creative juices and get them flowing again. So, to one and all: Drink freely, then leave behind a cup or two for those who are running dry. ~ Phil

Appreciation

I am grateful to my beloved wife, Kathy, for her tireless patience, help, and support as my partner in ministry, not only in preparing this book for publication but in all phases of life. As a Master Life Bible scholar, she has been my sparring partner on many occasions, challenging my view of scripture and adding to it insights and Bible references I had overlooked. She has been a blessing not only to me, but to all those congregations we have served over the years, reaching out to parishioners in quiet ways of compassionate, devotion, and love.

I am also grateful to my longtime friend, Elena See, who has received my sermons by email for years and, on several occasions, has prompted me to select a few keepers to share with the public. *Prime for the Pump* would not have come to be if not for her gentle prodding.

Foreword

Once upon a time, out in the Armargosa Desert, about 100 miles west of Indian Springs, Nevada, there lived an old prospector named "Desert Pete." For years he'd lived all alone in a run-down shack along the banks of a dried-up creek bed. As the story goes, ole Desert Pete was among the last remnant of the great California gold rush who, once the gold fever cooled down, stayed on and toughened in the heat of the blazing sun and scorching sand. To the curious on-looker, Desert Pete may have appeared callous and foreboding, what with his scraggly long beard, his crusty hands and face, and his ever-squinting, beady little eyes peering from beneath the brim of his old, tattered hat. But to many a lost, weary traveler, Desert Pete was an angel sent from God, for beside that old shack of his was a well with an old-timey hand pump that gushed forth with the coolest, sweetest, most succulent water you've ever tasted in your life. Far from being a forbidden habitat, Desert Pete's little homestead was an oasis to be sought for refreshment, rest, and renewal. As the years went by, time began to tell on old Desert Pete. His strength began to wane, his stamina good for only a few hours in the cool of the morning and the late afternoon. Then one day he was gone, never to be seen or heard from again. Some said distant relatives had taken him into Phoenix to live in a nursing home. Others said he just wandered off like an old dog that knows she's about to die. No one quite knew for sure. But those who came upon his place found in his absence the spirit of Desert Pete, alive and well, for wired to the handle of that old pump was a baking soda can. Inside the can was a note scribbled out in pencil by ole Desert Pete himself. The note read:

> "Pump working as of June 4, 1932. New sucker washer installed this date. Ought to last 5 years or more. Washer must be wet, and pump primed in order to work. Under the big white rock at your feet, I buried a crock jar of water. DON'T DRINK IT! Pour in about a fourth to soak the leather, then pour in the rest medium fast and pump as fast as you can. You'll git all the water you need. Signed, Desert Pete. P.S. When you've drunk your fill, don't forget to fill the jar for the next feller to come along."

PART ONE

Stories

I love old preacher stories. They've been around forever. Somehow, they've gotten passed down from one generation to the next. Most are quaint, some are true, others contrived and unlikely enough to be taken seriously for anything other than a simple story that is easy for others to visualize and get the point. A parable, in other words.

Since they're handed down verbally through sermons and word of mouth, there can be any number of variations. Here's one example:

> "Back in 1918, a boy named Howard Loomis was abandoned by his mother at Father Flanagan's Home for Boys, which had opened just a year earlier. Howard

had polio and wore heavy leg braces. Walking was difficult for him, especially when he had to go up or down steps. Soon, several of the Home's older boys were carrying Howard up and down the stairs. One day, Father Flanagan asked Rueben Granger, one of the older boys, if carrying Howard was hard. Rueben replied, 'He ain't heavy, Father, he's my brother.'" (*www.boys town.org.*)

For the record, Rev. James Wells used "an almost identical expression" in his book, *The Parables of Jesus*, published in 1884, thirty-four years earlier. Preacher stories are like that. They get passed around.

Preachers tend to collect preacher stories like fishermen collect lures. You can never get enough. One might be just what a decent sermon needs to bring it home at the end. I've selected the following preacher stories to illustrate the "prime for the pump", knowing from experience how the average preacher, teacher, student often needs to fan the cooling embers of inspiration with a warm glow of thoughtful devotion and praise. I hope you enjoy them.

I Am Your Path

E. Stanley Jones, renowned 20th Century missionary/evangelist, tells the story of a missionary who got hopelessly lost in a jungle in Africa. He wandered aimlessly for hours until he happened upon a small tribal village. Luckily, the chieftain spoke English. The missionary explained where he'd come from and asked if someone could help him find his way home. "I will take you there," the chieftain said. So, they set out walking through the jungle, hacking away the underbrush as they went. After several hours, the missionary said, "I still don't see a path." The chieftain smiled and said, "Bwana, I am your path."

Every major religion offers a path to salvation. For Taoism, it's the Tao. For Judaism, it's the Torah. For Islam, it's the Koran. For Christianity, it's the Old and New Testaments of the Bible, the inspired Word of God.

But it's more than that. Beyond the written words of the Bible is the pre-existent Word of God, who was with God in the beginning (Genesis 1:1) and made himself known as one of us in the person of Jesus of Nazareth. Jesus' teaching and example, along with the inspiration of his Holy Spirit, combine to give us clarity, direction, and purpose to live by faith, leading to the goal of peace, joy, and love in the realm of God's eternal kingdom.

Jesus told his disciples, "I am the way, the truth, and the life, no one comes to the Father but by me." *(John 14:6 RSV)* His way is not a path that can be plotted and charted on a map and defined by a system of religion and theology. It can only be found in the experience of looking in faith to him and trusting his Spirit to lead the way, one step at a time.

Are You Saved?

An enthusiastic young evangelist once asked an Amish farmer, "Mister, are you saved?" The farmer replied, "Why would you ask me such a question as that? Why, I could tell you anything." Then, reaching into the pocket of his bib overalls, he brought out a little spiral notebook and said, "Look, here are the names of my workers who prepare the fields, plant the seeds and harvest the crops. This is my banker who lends me money, this is the grocer who buys my produce, and this is the owner of the feed store where I buy my seed and fertilizer. Ask them if I am saved."

Jesus warned his disciples, "Beware of false prophets, who come to you in sheep's clothing but inwardly are ravenous wolves. You will know them by their fruits." *(Matthew 7:15-16 RSV.)* What does it mean to be saved? It's to know the promise of eternal life through faith in Jesus Christ. As importantly, it's to experience life in abundance as you live by faith, day by day, guided by his teachings and example, loving your neighbor as yourself and living in charity with others, welcoming strangers, and befriending those in need.

Healthy Distancing

The story is told of a woman watching a butterfly emerge from a cocoon. It bit and tore at the shell as it struggled to break free. The process seemed to take forever. More than once, the chrysalis seemed to become exhausted and give up, only to revive its strength and try again. As she watched, she couldn't help but feel sorry for the poor creature, so she got a pair of cuticle scissors and carefully snipped the walls of the cocoon. Just like that, the butterfly popped out and began stretching its wings. But it lacked the strength to fly. She realized, only after it was too late, that the fierce struggle to get out of the cocoon was necessary for the butterfly to develop the strength and stamina it would need to survive. By doing for the butterfly what it needed to do for itself, she crippled it for life.

This is one of the hardest lessons for parents to put into practice: Letting the children solve their own problems, find the answers for themselves, make their own decisions. The temptation is to make life easier for them by picking up the toys, "helping" with their homework, or giving them extra spending money rather than insisting that they do something to earn the money or learn to do without.

It's sad, but true: Whether relating to children or adults, doing for others what they can do for themselves makes them weaker and more dependent on others.

Jesus knew this lesson well. One of the turning points in training his disciples came when he cut them loose and sent them out on their own. Luke writes,

> "When Jesus had called the Twelve together, he gave them power and authority to drive out all demons and to cure diseases, and he sent them out to proclaim the kingdom of God and to heal the sick." *(Luke 9:1-2 NIV)*

More importantly, when the time was right, he left them on their own for good. Why? He said, "Unless I go away, the Advocate will not come to you; but if I go, I will send him to you." *(John 16:7 NIV)*

It was part of God's plan: while Jesus was with them, day after day, they would depend on him to lead the way. Only after he was gone would they muster the courage to decide for themselves where to go and what to do; only after he was gone would they speak and act on the strength of their own faith and conviction; only after they felt the void of his absence would they experience the power of his presence as a gift of the Holy Spirit.

The Blessing of a Burden

We all know what it's like to carry a burden. For example, to be critically injured in a major accident is to undergo extensive rehabilitation, to treat a life-threatening disease is to be strapped with a mountain of medical bills; to buy a home is to make monthly payments for years to come.

This was the recurring theme of a popular TV series in the mid-50's called, *The Millionaire*. For no apparent reason, a wealthy benefactor would choose a struggling couple and have his valet show up at their doorstep and deliver an anonymous check for one million dollars, no strings attached.

At first, it felt too good to be true. Their burdens were lifted, just like that. They were now free to pursue their fondest dreams. But, as reality set in, they quickly found themselves at odds with each other and at a loss as to knowing how to manage such a staggering sum of money in a meaningful way. The gift resulted in being their worst nightmare, not their dream-come-true. Thankfully, burdens can also be a blessing.

The story is told of a missionary in Africa who was desperately trying to return to his village. It was the monsoon season, and the creeks and rivers were swollen and flooding. He came to a small river separating him from his family and stopped in his tracks. The current was far too swift for him to get across without being swept away. A local tribesman saw his plight and came to help. Without a word, the tribesman took the largest boulder he could carry, put it on his shoulder, and waded out into the water. The weight of the stone gave him the ballast he needed to keep his balance. The missionary followed his example and was home in no time. The experience taught him that, often, the burdens we carry are just what we need to stay grounded.

Going back to Father Flanagan and Rueben Grainger's comment, *"He ain't heavy, he's my brother,"* we all know how some burdens are easier to bear than others. Why is that? I can think of two reasons: The relationship of the person bearing the burden to the one needing a helping hand, and the freedom to choose otherwise.

In other words, it's easier to help your brother or sister than a total stranger or someone you are at odds with. The closer a loving relationship, the lighter the load. It's also important to have the freedom to choose to bear the burdens of others as opposed to feeling obligated: The greater the freedom, the lighter the load. Either way, Paul admonishes us, "Bear one another's burdens, and so fulfil the law of Christ." *(Galatians 6:2 RSV)*

Turning to Jesus gives us the strength and willing heart we need to help others bear the burdens of life. As Jesus told his disciples, "Come to me, all who labor and are heavy laden, and I will give you rest. Take my yoke upon you and learn from me; for I am gentle and lowly in heart, and you will find rest for your souls, for my yoke is easy, and my burden is light." *(Matthew 11:28-30 RSV)*

The Spirit of Adoption

I'm reminded of the story of a teacher who was welcoming two new students to her class. They said they were brothers. "How old are you?" she asked. Both answered at once, "Seven." "Are you twins?" she asked. One answered, "No ma'am, my birthday is April 8. My brother's birthday is April 20." "So," the teacher asked, "Are you stepbrothers?" The other replied, "No ma'am, one of us is adopted." Out of curiosity, she asked, "Which one?" They grinned and said, "We asked our mother, but she said she loved us so much she couldn't remember."

I don't know of a better way to think of our relationship to God than adoption. As Paul said to the Romans:

> "For those who are led by the Spirit of God are the children of God. The Spirit does not make you a slave … but brings about your adoption as a child of God." … And if we are God's children, we are heirs of God and co-heirs with Christ, provided we share in his sufferings." *(Romans 8:14-17 NIV)*

Years ago, there lived a couple in West Texas who adopted two children, a boy and a girl, from the Edna Gladney home in Fort Worth. From day one, they wanted their children to know that they were chosen, not just picked at random. So, in addition to celebrating their birthdays, they also celebrated their children's "Gotcha Day," the day they picked them up from the orphanage and brought them to their home to live. But they didn't stop there. They went on to emphasize how God had chosen them to be part of his great family of faith through the atoning death and resurrection of Jesus Christ.

Think of how this might speak to you: Of all the people on earth, God picked you and called you his own. As Paul told the Ephesians, "For it is by grace you have been saved, through faith—and this is not from yourselves, it is the gift of God— not by works, so that no one can boast." *(Ephesians 2:8-9 NIV).*

Jesus told his disciples, "You did not choose me, but I chose you and appointed you so that you might go and bear fruit" (John 15:16 NIV). As followers of Jesus, we are members of God's great family of faith by adoption. Knowing this, the least we can do is love one another as brothers and sisters in Christ and live in such a way as to become "the spitting image" of our Father.

If You Can Lead Me to the Cross

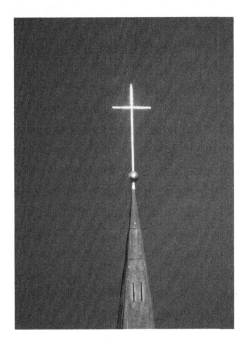

One of my favorite stories is of the little boy who moved to a big city with his mother and little sister. His mother found a job and rented an apartment near an old church with a lighted cross towering high above the steeple. Adventuresome, the little nine-year-old soon explored the neighborhood and began finding his way around. As adventuresome boys will do, he ventured farther and farther from home until, one day, he got lost.

He wandered this way and that, trying to retrace his steps, but no matter how hard he tried, he became even more disoriented, then it started to get dark, and the streetlights came on. To add to his misery, it started to sprinkle, and, in no time, he was cold and wet. Not knowing what else to do, he sat on a curb and started to cry.

Just then, a police officer came along. He stooped down and asked the little boy his name and where he lived. The little boy told the officer his name, but he couldn't remember the name of the street he lived on or the apartment number. The officer encouraged him to remember what he could, and the little boy smiled and said, "There's a big church next door, and it's got this cross on top that lights up the whole neighborhood at night. If you can lead me to the cross, I can find my way home." Once he saw the light of the cross shining from the church next door, he would be home free.

His comment gives us an example of "unconscious prophecy," saying something profound without realizing the deeper implications. As a child, he had no way of knowing how his words might later speak to others of the death and resurrection of Jesus.

Another example of unconscious prophecy is the time the Jewish Council debated what to do with Jesus. The high priest, Caiaphas, told them: "You know nothing at all; you do not understand that it is expedient for you that one man should die for the people, and that the whole nation should not perish." (John 11:49-50 RSV). For now, let's give the little boy the credit he's due: To see the light of the cross is to know the promise of new life in Jesus Christ ever calling you home.

To Give Your Life for a Friend

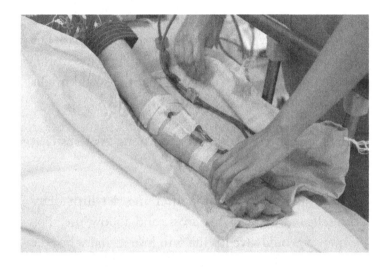

Once there lived a ten-year-old named Liz who suffered from a rare and deadly blood disease. As it happened, her little brother, Tim, age five, had survived the disease and had developed the antibodies necessary to combat the infection. Liz's only hope of survival was for Tim to donate his blood. Their mother explained the situation to Tim and asked, "Are you willing to donate your blood to save your sister's life?" Tim thought about, it, took a deep breath, and said, "Yes." The nurses quickly went to work and, in no time, started the transfusion. As the little boy watched the blood flowing from his vein into the bag below, he asked his mother, "Will I die right away, or will it take a while?" Being so young, Tim didn't know they were only going to take a pint of blood. He thought they were asking him to give up his life to save the life of his sister, and the beauty of it all is that he said yes.

One of the most important teachings of Jesus was the Love Command: "Love one another as I have loved you." *(John 15:12 RSV)* He went on to say, "Greater love has no one than this: to lay down one's life for one's friends." *(John 15:13 RSV)* But he didn't stop there. He went on to teach by example, laying down his life for the sins of the world. In the words of John's gospel:

> "For God so loved the world that he gave his only Son, that whoever believes in him shall not perish but have eternal life. For God sent the Son into the world, not to condemn the world, but that the world might be saved through him." (John 3:16-17 RSV)

The challenge is to follow in his footsteps. As Jesus charged his followers:

> "If any man would come after me, let him deny himself and take up his cross, and follow me. For whoever would save his life will lose it: and whoever loses his life for my sake will find it." *(Matthew 16:24-25 RSV)*

Take this home with you: To die to self is to experience the fullness of life Jesus promised to all who put their faith in him. *(John 10:10).*

Are You Rich?

They huddled just outside the door. Two children in ragged outgrown coats. "Any old papers, lady?" they asked. I was busy. I wanted to say no. Then I looked at their feet. Thin little sandals sopped with snow and rain. "Come in and I'll see," I said, "but first sit down and I'll make you a cup of hot cocoa." They said nothing. Their big wide eyes spoke for them. As they walked to the fireplace and sat down their soggy sandals left a trail on the carpet. I shook my head and went into the kitchen.

Cocoa and toast with jam to fortify children against the cold outside. I left them to look for old papers. As I gathered the papers, I walked past the living room slowly, better to observe my guests as I passed. They sat in silence. The little girl held her empty cup in her hands, looking at it wistfully. The little boy saw me in the hallway and asked flatly, "Lady, are you rich?" "Am I rich? Mercy no!" I exclaimed. I looked at my well-worn furniture and somewhat faded draperies and repeated emphatically, "I surely am not rich!"

The little girl put her cup back in its saucer carefully. "Your cups match your saucers," she said. Her voice was older than her years. It spoke of a hunger not of the stomach. I handed them each a small bundle of papers. As they left, they held them tightly against the cold, gusty wind. They had not said thank-you. They had said much more. Plain blue pottery cups and saucers. But they matched.

I tasted the potatoes and stirred the gravy. Potatoes and brown gravy. A roof over our heads. My husband with a steady job. These matched as well. I moved the chairs back from the fireplace and tidied the room somewhat. The muddy prints of small sandals were still wet on the carpet and hearth. I let them be. They were the children's gift to me. A reminder just in case I ever forget just how rich I truly am.

Many Gifts, All One Body, We

Once upon a time, the tools in a carpenter's toolbox got into a squabble. The square complained that the hammer was too loud. The hammer complained that the pencil always needed to be sharpened. The pencil complained that the screwdriver had to be turned round and round to get any work done. The screwdriver complained that the plane was shallow, that his work lacked proper depth. The plane complained that the ruler was always trying to decide who measured up. The ruler complained that the sandpaper rubbed people the wrong way. Then the carpenter came in, put on his apron, and went to work.

One by one, he picked up the various tools and, with skilled hands, crafted a beautiful piece of furniture. That evening the tools said nothing. They realized, as different as they were, each had an important part to play, that in the hands of the master carpenter, each was essential to the task.

The Apostle Paul was a tentmaker, not a carpenter, but he knew the importance of working together, of cooperating instead of competing. He thought of the church as the visible body of Christ in the world today. He told the Corinthians:

> "Just as a body, though one, has many parts, but all its many parts are one body, so it is with Christ. For we were all baptized by one Spirit to form one body—whether Jews or Gentiles, slave or free—and we were all given the one Spirit to drink. Even so the body is not made up of one part but of many. Now if the foot should say, 'Because I am not a hand, I do not belong to the body,' it would not for that reason stop being part of the body. And if the ear should say, 'Because I am not an eye, I do not belong to the body,' it would not for that reason stop being part of the body. If the whole body were an eye, where would the sense of hearing be? If the whole body were an ear, where would the sense of smell be? But in fact, God has placed the parts in the body, every one of them, just as he wanted them to be. If they were all one part, where would the body be? As it is, there are many parts, but one body. Now you are the body of Christ, and each one of you is a part of it. If one part suffers, every part suffers with it; if one part is honored, every part rejoices with it." (1 Corinthians 12:12-27 NIV)

As you seek to follow his example, remember his words: "… you are the body of Christ." So are all who put their trust in him. Dare to live together in the unity of his spirit. Lose your yourself in service of the common good. Work together in such a way as to build up the church and bring honor and glory to Jesus Christ.

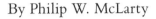

A Lily Bulb Named Betty Lou

By Philip W. McLarty

Once upon a time there lived a lily bulb named Betty Lou. Betty Lou lived, along with several dozen lily bulbs, in a tray in the greenhouse of the Hastings Lawn and Garden Store. As a bulb, Betty Lou led a happy, carefree life. She was plump and pretty, and she got along well with all the other bulbs. But she had one horrible fear: Betty Lou did not want to be planted. It was like an obsession to her. Just thinking about it gave her nightmares.

Eddie, one of the other bulbs in the tray, told stories of what being planted would be like. "First, you get all soggy," he said, "Then your outer layer starts to decay, and there's nothing you can do to stop it. It's all dark and cold, and you just rot away until there's nothing left of you at all." "Yuck!" Betty Lou said with a shiver. "Why can't others just leave me alone and appreciate me as I am?"

One day, a bulb named Sis spoke up. "It won't be long now," she said. The other bulbs listened carefully because Sis was always right. "It won't be long until folks start coming in to pick us over," Sis said. "I've seen it happen to the Azaleas already. We're all going to be planted soon." "Oh, God!" Betty Lou prayed, "Don't let that happen to me!"

Sure enough, just as Sis predicted, customers started coming into the store. When they came to the lilies, they grabbed up a handful of bulbs and put them in a sack, not even looking them over as carefully as you might an apple or an onion. Betty Lou felt secure, being tucked away in a corner under a couple of larger bulbs. Still, she was afraid.

One day, about six weeks before Easter, Mrs. Hastings called to her gardener, "George, get some pots and plant the rest of those lily bulbs. We'll be getting calls for Easter lilies before we know it." George grabbed a handful of pots and filled them with soil. But George had grabbed up one pot too few, and when he came to Betty Lou, now all alone in the corner of the tray, there were no more pots close by. So, he just grabbed Betty Lou, looked around, and stuck her up on a high shelf where no one could see her. And there, high on the shelf, overlooking the whole greenhouse, Betty Lou sat. All alone.

At first, she breathed a sigh of relief. Then she began to look around. "What a magnificent view!" she said. "I didn't know what I was missing." And, for a while, Betty Lou enjoyed her place on the shelf with her excellent view. And her solitary life. Being a bulb - regardless of how plump and pretty - didn't feel nearly as good as it once had.

Just as Betty Lou was about to break down and cry, Mrs. Hastings came in. "Where on earth could I have left that trowel?" she wondered. She stood on a box to reach the top shelf. As her hand bumped into Betty Lou, she exclaimed, "What have we here?" She grabbed an empty pot, filled it with soil and planted the bulb.

"You'll never make it by Easter," she said, "but I tell you what, if nobody else wants you, I'll take you home with me for Mother's Day." In that instant, Betty Lou, the lily bulb, died, and Betty Lou, the magnificent lily, was born.

The Legend of the Dandelion

By Philip W. McLarty

Not long after Jesus had been raised from the dead, the spring flowers got together for a meeting. They felt it only proper that one of them should serve as a reminder of the hope of new life for all. So, they met together in the middle of a lovely garden. A Daffodil popped up first. "I think I should be the flower picked to symbolize the resurrection," she said. "After all, I am the first to arrive in the spring. If you ask me, that fits the image of the Son of God." The other flowers considered her opinion but didn't say a word.

Finally, the Tulip spoke up. "Yes, it is true, you are the first to arrive. No one can deny that. But, if I may speak freely, you are much too foolhardy for your own good, for there are times when a late frost comes and nips you in the bud. The Son of God comes in His own due time." She lowered her bloom in a respectful, but firm, manner. A quiet murmur of agreement circulated among the other flowers.

Now there were, spotted among this beautiful array of flowers, a few scraggly Dandelions, hardly noticeable to anyone. About this time, a puff of wind stirred through the flowers, scattering the blooms of the Dandelions to the nearby fields.

A group of Pansies spoke up. "We are much too prim and dainty to represent the Son of God. So are the Daisies and the Periwinkles and the Violets, for that matter. But there is one among us who fits the image perfectly. Her bloom is elegant. What's more, she is embedded in thorns, just as the son of God wore a crown of thorns. The Rose is the proper symbol of the resurrection," they said. The flowers stirred with excitement. They all agreed the Rose was an object of beauty. And the thorns of its stem were most appropriate. Some of the flowers were eager to cast their vote. Meanwhile, another gust of wind braced the garden and more Dandelion blooms were blown away to fields unknown.

It was the tall, stately Iris who quieted the stir. "The Rose is, without doubt, one of the loveliest of the flowers," she said, "And its thorns are a fitting reminder of the crown placed upon our Lord's brow. But the Rose does not stand alone. It lacks a certain sturdiness and independence, preferring instead, to be bunched with others, sometime in a variety of colors." The Azaleas nodded in agreement.

The Iris continued, "The symbol of our Lord and His resurrection from the dead must be one who is stately and strong, one who rises above the common plant and stands alone to herald His coming." Gesturing toward the center of the garden, she said, "The Lily most perfectly is qualified to be our symbol."

The other flowers in the garden turned in deference to the

Lily and blushed with humility. The Lily stood out among them; unpretentious, but elegant, and gracious beyond compare.

Another gust of wind bristled the garden, taking with it the remaining Dandelion blooms. As for the Lily, it swayed gracefully in the breeze, undaunted and unafraid.

"Are there others we have overlooked?" a Gardenia asked. The flowers looked around. No one noticed the abandoned Dandelion stems, but then, it wouldn't have mattered if they had. The Dandelion was the least—and most unlovely—of all the flowers. A mere weed to be trodden under foot, yet reminiscent of Jesus, "… who was wounded for our transgressions and bruised for our iniquities …" Isaiah 53:5 (RSV)

"We're ready to cast our vote," spoke the Petunias. "So are we!" added the Lilacs. The other flowers agreed as well. It was unanimous. The Lily would serve as a reminder of the hope of new life for all to see in the springtime of each new year. And so, from that day forth, it has been known as the *"Easter Lily."*

The flowers adjourned; confident they had made the right choice. Meanwhile, the Dandelion seeds, now scattered far and wide, began to break open and take root, waiting for their chance next spring, perhaps on Easter Sunday, to pop up and announce the glad tidings: "The Lord is risen; He is risen indeed!" And if others did not happen to notice the children picking their stems and blowing their balls of seeds to the four winds, what difference would it make? There would be another year—another spring—and that many more Dandelions to join their unending chorus.

PART TWO

Sermons

What is a sermon?

The Merriam-Webster dictionary defines a sermon as, "... a religious discourse delivered in public usually by a member of the clergy as a part of a worship service." *(https://www.merriam-webster. com/dictionary/sermon.*

In the Christian faith, a sermon is more narrowly understood as the proclamation of God's Word based on the authority of the scriptures of the Old and New Testaments. To proclaim God's Word is to speak for God by the inspiration of the Holy Spirit.

Sermons come in all shapes and sizes. Two common types of sermons include Expository Sermons and Topical Sermons. Expository sermons seek to expose the truth of God's Word as expressed in a particular passage of the Bible. Topical Sermons seek to address how scripture speaks to a particular topic of the day – prayer in public schools, for example. Topical sermons would also include the countless sermons delivered on the evening of September 11, 2001, as preachers from all over the United States responded to the terrorist attack on New York City and the Pentagon and sought to answer the question on the minds and hearts of worshipers, "Is there a word from the Lord?"

The two most common forms of sermons are oral sermons and written sermons. Oral sermons are spoken with a minimum of notes.

Written sermons range from manuscripts to be read to expanded notes to keep the preacher on topic.

The goal of every sermon is to tell the truth of God's Word within the understanding of the listener. Ideally, the "miracle of preaching" is that sermons speak the truth of God's Word, despite the limitations of the preacher and the limited faith and understanding of the listener.

How does this work? Here's what I think: In the process of preaching and listening to a sermon, the Spirit of God in the preacher communicates with the Spirit of God in the listener in such a way as to convey God's Word, even though what the listener professes to have heard is not necessarily the same as what the preacher professes to have said.

Following are a few of my sermons from the past, edited and abbreviated for inclusion in this book. In sharing them with you, I pray that the Spirit may inspire you to hear God's Word and give you the courage to speak for the Lord by the inspiration of the Holy Spirit.

His Master's Voice

John 10:1-6

I brought a couple of pictures to show you this morning. The first is a painting by Francis Barraud entitled, *"His Master's Voice."* You'll recognize it as the RCA logo.

The dog's name is Nipper. His original master was Francis' brother, Mark Barraud. When Mark died in 1887, Francis took Nipper to live with him. Nipper was fascinated by the newly invented cylinder phonograph. He could hear the sound of music and voices, but he couldn't figure out where they were coming from. He'd tilt his head to one side, then the other, listening to the sounds and trying to resolve the mystery. It inspired Francis to think of how Nipper might react if he were to hear Mark's voice coming from the Gramophone. So, he painted Nipper faithfully sitting there in front of the speaker listening for his master's voice.

The second picture is of my ten-year-old Dachshund, Ginger.

Like Nipper, Ginger knows her master's voice. She listens to me when I talk to her. She comes to me when I call her name. She knows she can depend on me to look out for her, and she trusts me to take good care of her.

She relates easily to just about everybody, but, even when she's in the middle of a crowded room with everyone talking at once, all I have to say is, "Come, Ginger," and she'll come running. So, it's little wonder that I think of Ginger and this old painting by Francis Barraud when I hear Jesus' words,

"... the sheep hear the shepherd's voice. He calls them by name and leads them out (of the sheepfold) ... he goes ahead of them, and they follow him, because they know his voice." (*John 10:3-4 RSV*)

Let's think about what it means to listen for the voice of Jesus. What does the Master's voice sound like, and how are we to distinguish his voice from all the competing voices in our world today? How can we make sure the voice we're listening to is Jesus' voice and not that of thieves and robbers? Finally, what are some of the ways we can fine tune our receivers to filter out some of the noise and static and interference of this chaotic world in which we live?

To begin, let's be clear, there have always been other voices competing for our attention. As one commentator put it, "Despite twenty centuries of warning, the church continues to have difficulty discerning a thief in the sheepfold." *(Preaching Through the Christian Year, Craddock, Tucker, Holladay, et al., Year A, p. 269)* It was just as confusing in Jesus' day. Jesus said,

> "Beware of false prophets, who come to you in sheep's clothing but inwardly are ravenous wolves." *(Matthew 7:15 RSV)* To the Ephesians, Paul said, "I know that after I have gone, savage wolves will come in among you, not sparing the flock. Some even from your own group will come distorting the truth to entice the disciples to follow them. Therefore, be alert!" *(Acts 20:29-31 NIV)*

Who are you going to listen to, and how can you be sure the voice you're listening to is the Master's voice and not that of a thief or robber? What are the distinguishing traits of Jesus' voice? My list is not exhaustive, but as a start, the voice of Jesus is gentle, not overbearing. He says things like,

> "Come to me, all who labor and are heavy-laden, and I will give you rest. Take my yoke upon you and learn from me, for I am gentle and lowly in heart, and you will find rest for your souls. For my yoke is easy, and my burden is light." *(Matthew 11:28-30 RSV)*

Jesus is not one to impose himself on you, but to invite you graciously to come into his presence. He says, "Behold, I stand at the door and knock, if anyone hears my voice and opens the door, I will come into him and eat with him and he with me." (Revelation 3:20 RSV)

Jesus' voice is sympathetic and understanding. Scripture says, "As he went ashore, he saw a great crowd; and he had compassion for them, because they were like sheep without a shepherd; and he began to teach them many things." *(Mark 6:34 RSV)*

The voice of Jesus is forgiving. A woman was brought to him who had been caught in the act of adultery. The religious leaders asked him whether she should be stoned to death, and he responded saying, "He who is without sin among you be the first to throw a stone at her, and they all went away." (*John 8:7 RSV*) Then he said to the woman, "Neither do I condemn you; go, and do not sin again." (*John 8:10-11 RSV*)

He taught his disciples to forgive each other, not seven times, as the law prescribed, but *"seventy times seven,"* in other words, as many times as necessary. (*Matthew 18:21-22*)

More than anything, the voice of Jesus is loving. He said, "You shall love the Lord your God with all your heart and with all your soul, and with all your mind, and you shall love your neighbor as yourself." (*Matthew 22:37-39 RSV*)

This was the first and greatest of the commandments. He taught his disciples to love one another, as he had loved them. (*John 15:12*) He also taught them to love their enemies and pray for those who persecuted them. (*Matthew 5:44*)

Jesus could be critical, to be sure, especially when it came to matters of false piety and self-righteousness. For example, he said, "Judge not, that you not be judged. For with the judgment you pronounce you will be judged, and the measure you give will be the measure you get." (*Matthew 7:1-2 RSV*) He overturned the moneychangers' tables in the temple, saying, "My house shall be a house of prayer, but you make it a den of robbers." (*Matthew 21:13 RSV*)

His most scathing words were directed to the scribes and Pharisees. He said, "The scribes and Pharisees sit on Moses' seat; so practice and observe what they tell you, but not what they do, for they preach, but do not practice (what they preach). They bind heavy burdens, hard to bear and lay them on men's shoulders, but they themselves will not move them with their finger." (*Matthew 23:3-5 RSV*) He went on to say, "Woe to you, scribes and Pharisees, hypocrites!" ... "for you are like whitewashed tombs, which outwardly appear beautiful, but within they are full of dead men's bones and all uncleanness." (*Matthew 23:27-28 RSV*)

Yes, Jesus could be harsh, but for the most part, he was gracious and kind and understanding, never ceasing to share the Good News of God's love with others. Even from the Cross, he told the repentant thief who hung beside him, "Truly, I say to you, today you will be with me in Paradise." (*Luke 23:43 RSV*)

This is only a representative example of Jesus' words. There are many more sayings of Jesus, and I encourage you to read the gospels for yourself and make your own list. As you do, listen to the sound of Jesus' words. Rehearse his teachings over and over until his voice stands out over all the many competing voices vying for your attention.

Scripture is one sure way to hear the Master's voice, but there are at least two other ways, and I'd like to mention them briefly. One is the voice of conscience; the other, the witness of others. When we prayerfully listen for the inspiration of God's voice, God speaks to us through the voice of conscience. As children, we are taught to let the voice of conscience tell us right from wrong. As we grow older, the voice of conscience helps us make sound ethical and moral decisions. If a friend was wrestling with an issue, we would say, "Let your conscience be your guide." It was a pretty good rule-of-thumb: If you're true to your conscience, you're likely to be faithful to God.

God speaks to us through the voice of conscience; God also speaks to us through the witness of others. Others don't always agree, of course, so we must be careful not to put too much stock in what others say. But if we're willing to listen and consider other perspectives – especially if we're well-grounded in the scripture – God can use the witness of others to help us know the truth more fully and to follow his will for our lives. We can sift through the verbiage to lift out valuable insights and nuggets of truth while discarding that which is overly tainted and biased.

The bottom line is this: Jesus Christ is Lord. He's the shepherd of the flock. It's his voice we're to listen to, follow, and obey. The more we study his teachings in scripture, the more we turn to him in prayer, the more we listen to the wisdom of godly saints, the more likely we are to hear his voice over the chaos and clamor of the world in which we live. In closing, I invite you to let the words of this old gospel song speak to you,

"I come to the garden alone, while the dew is still on the roses, and the voice I hear falling on my ear, the Son of God discloses. And he walks with me, and he talks with me, and he tells me I am his own. And the joy we share as we tarry there none other has ever known."

May I Wash Your Feet?

John 13:4-5

May I wash your feet? We're on our feet a lot. If you were to think how it would feel to have someone wash your feet, you might be tempted to say yes. On the other hand, you might say no. There's a certain intimacy about feet. Most of us would be uncomfortable having someone wash our feet. Be that as it may, foot washing is a profound act of humility, and it captures the essence of Jesus' ministry:

> "Jesus ... rose from supper, laid aside his garments, and girded himself with a towel. Then he poured water into a basin and began to wash the disciples' feet, and to wipe them with the towel with which he was girded." (*John 13:4-5 RSV*).

To accept Jesus is to humble yourself and receive his sacrifice of love and devotion. To follow Jesus is to take up a basin and towel and humbly wash the feet of others.

I once served on the staff of a rescue mission in North Texas. We served three meals a day and offered overnight housing for transients. I was assisting the director check in the men for the night when one of the men walked in and said, "I got a sore foot, doc." The director told him to take a seat, and he'd look at his feet after he got everyone got signed in.

When the registration desk cleared, we walked down the hall

to the dispensary. The director sat on the cold, linoleum floor and began unlacing the man's boots. I pulled up a chair to watch and learn. The director untied his boots and gently peeled them off the man's feet. The room quickly filled with a pungent odor. He unfurled the socks, exposing festering blisters on both feet. Then he took a plastic tub from under the lavatory, filled it with warm water and added a generous portion of bacterial soap, then he took a clean, white towel from the drawer, put it around his neck and sat back down on the floor. The man slipped his feet into the tub of warm water and breathed a sigh of relief as he swished the water around his feet and let the Betadine do its work.

The director repeated the process three times, emptying the basin and filling it with fresh water. He took the towel and patted the man's feet dry then applied a coat of Neosporin to each blister. He then found a fresh pair of white athletic socks and slipped them on the man's feet. "Wear these tonight," he said, "and check back with me in the morning."

The man stood up and said, "You sure know what you're doing, doc. Where'd you learn how to wash feet like that?" The director looked up and said, "I had a good teacher. When you come back tomorrow, I'd like to tell you about him."

The question is, are you willing to follow Jesus' example? Are you willing to look a stranger in the eye – better yet, someone you are at odds with – and ask, *May I wash your feet?*

A Six-Volt Battery in a Twelve-Volt World

Today's sermon begins with a brief lesson in auto mechanics. In the old days – we're talking the 30s, 40s and 50s – cars came equipped with a six-volt electrical system. That's all they needed. The engines were small and there were few accessories – a starter (you had to crank the old Model T by hand), windshield wipers, and, if you were in tall cotton, an AM radio.

As cars got bigger and more powerful and loaded with accessories, the six-volt system couldn't handle the load. So, automakers switched over to a twelve-volt system, and it proved to be the ticket. Even the big SUVs today run on a twelve-volt system.

So, that's your automotive lesson for today. The reason I mention it is because, years ago, one of my best friends, frustrated with his wife's unwillingness to embrace new technology, railed out at her and said, "You're just a six-volt battery in a twelve-volt world."

That remark has stayed with me through the years, and it leads me to wonder: *Am I a six-volt battery in a twelve-volt world? Are you?* The gospel lesson for today brought this to mind:

> "Those who love their life lose it, and those who hate their life in this world will keep it for eternal life." (*John 12:25 RSV*)

As followers of Jesus Christ, we're to let go of the old and embrace the new. As Isaiah said, "Remember not the former things nor consider the things of old. Behold, I am doing a new thing; now it springs forth, do you not perceive it?" *(Isaiah 43:18-19 RSV)*

The problem is it's hard to know what to hold on to and what to let go of – how to cherish the faith of your fathers and mothers without getting stuck in the past; how to embrace new paradigms and expressions of faith without losing sight of where you've come from and where you're going.

I had a friend who worked in the service department of one of the big box stores in the mall. He described his work as a walk down memory lane. A customer would come in needing a part for an appliance. "Do you have the model number?" he'd ask. The customer would reply, "Can't you just look it up?" "Sorry," he'd say, "Without the make and model number, I can't find it in the computer."

The old system had worked well in the past. Why not modernize it and embrace new technology? Unspoken, the answer was, *"But we've never done it that way before!"*

We live in a changing world, and the question is when is it time to let go of the past and embrace new ways of thinking, and when is it wise to hold on to what we consider to be tried and true? Poet John Russell Lowell put it this way:

> "New occasions teach new duties; time makes ancient
> good uncouth. They must upward still and onward,
> who would keep abreast of truth."

The ordination service of the PC(USA) includes the question, "Do you sincerely receive and adopt the essential tenets of the Reformed faith as expressed in the confessions of our church?" *(The Book of Order, G-14.0405-3)*

I used to spend one whole session every year in Officer Training Class just trying to unpack this question. I'd show a twenty-minute videotape by a seminary professor explaining what is meant by the term, "essential tenets." It never failed; the newly elected elders would leave in a daze. So, if it's so difficult, why not drop this question? Answer: "ARE YOU KIDDING?!"

As you know, we offer a 12-week Confirmation Class every year for 7th and 8th graders. These kids are bright and eager to learn. Before they're confirmed, they can answer any number of Bible questions, tell you about the sacraments, and recite the Apostles' Creed and the Lord's Prayer. But are they equipped to withstand the forces of evil in the world today? Will they be able to hear God's Word over the clamor of the marketplace? Can they hold their own in the struggle between religious fundamentalism and secular humanism? Do they have what it takes to live a life of faith in a dot.com world? If we're not careful, we can go through the motions of keeping the faith of our fathers and mothers without experiencing the promise of new life in Jesus Christ.

What does it mean to cherish the faith without getting stuck in the past? What does it mean to embrace new paradigms and expressions of faith without losing sight of essential tenets and time-honored practices?

I'll be the first to confess I love the old traditions of the church. I love the great hymns of the faith like, *"Holy, Holy, Holy,"* and *"A Mighty Fortress Is Our God."* I love old gospel hymns like, *"Amazing Grace"* and *"The Old Rugged Cross."* Then there's the liturgy. I've sung the Doxology and the Gloria Patri ever since I can remember. I learned to say the Lord's Prayer and the Apostles' Creed by rote, even when I didn't know the meaning of all the words.

I love the old traditions, but new liturgy and new forms of music are emerging. Is there room for both? If we don't keep pace with the world in which we live; we quickly get out of touch; if we're too worldly, we lose our distinctive witness as people of God and disciples of Jesus Christ.

Is it possible to capture the best of both worlds? I once passed a caravan of pickup trucks on the Interstate pulling flatbed trailers carrying perfectly restored old cars. I'm guessing they were on their way to an antique car show. I passed slowly to get a good look. As I did, I took note of the fact that each flatbed trailer was being pulled by a late-model Dodge Hemi or Ford or Chevy Diesel.

How does this speak to you? As a grandfather, here's how it speaks to me: As far as my grandchildren are concerned, I'm the old guy who gets down on the floor and rides them around on his back. Little do they know, I'm also an old guy who's learning from them how to be a child again. Jesus said, "Unless you become as a child you can never enter the Kingdom of God." (18:17 RSV) My grandchildren are helping me embrace a new me.

As Pastor of this church, I'm challenged by the Korean congregation we invited to worship and fellowship with each other in Fellowship Hall on Sunday afternoons. I visit them often, and I see in them a spark of piety and devotion to God that used to characterize the church I remember as a child. They raise the roof with their singing. They bring in an evangelist twice a year to hold a revival. Plus, they have a small group of men who meet in the parlor every morning at 5:30 to pray. They're meek and gracious to a fault, but unrelenting when it comes to making disciples for the Lord Jesus Christ.

Then there are the Muslim students. You may not be aware of this, but we usually have one or two Muslim students attend the worship service with us every Sunday morning. They belong to the Interfaith Dialogue Students Association at Texas A&M. I often visit with them after church to discuss the similarities and differences of our faith. Getting to know them challenges me to think globally and look for common ground with people of other faiths.

These are three areas of my life in which I am slowly letting go of the old and embracing the new. No, I'm not going to be a child again, nor am I going to join the Korean congregation or convert to Islam. What I intend to do is shed those parts of my faith that are hackneyed and out of touch and replace them with new ways of walking in the footsteps of Jesus Christ. I think this is what Charles Wesley had in mind when he penned the words,

"A charge to keep I have, a God to glorify, A never-dying soul to save and fit it for the sky. To serve the present age, my calling to fulfill, O may it all my powers engage to do my Master's will."

To be faithful to Christ and his kingdom is to let go of who you are and let God transform you into what God would have you to become. Anything less is to be a six-volt battery in a twelve-volt world.

Gracias, Señor, Por Tu Gracia

¿Habla Español? Do you speak Spanish? It's worth trying, if for no other reason than to pick a few words and make the connection between Spanish and English. For example, in Spanish the word for "Thank you" is "Gracias." It comes from the same root as grace, "Gracia." To express one leads to the other; to be thankful is to say grace for gifts you've received.

This relationship of grace and gratitude lies at the heart of faith because the things for which we're most thankful reflect gifts of grace we don't necessarily deserve and over which we have little control.

When you ask, "What are you most grateful for?" many would say, "My health, my family, and my friends." You can't do better than these. Good health is something to be thankful for, especially when you consider there's no guarantee. You can eat healthy foods three meals a day, jog every morning, have a positive, winning attitude, get plenty of sleep and still be cut down in the prime of life.

One of the leading members of my church was a youthful, athletic, out-going, 53-year-old man. A non-smoker. An occasional social drinker. A family man. He got up one morning, went for his 3-mile run, came home, showered, felt dizzy and went to the hospital. The doctors and nurses couldn't find anything wrong with him, but, as a cautionary measure, they put him on telemetry and kept him overnight to monitor his vital signs. That night, he suffered a massive stroke and never recovered.

These things happen. Your health can be stripped away without warning, and it doesn't matter how much wheat germ and broccoli you've eaten. If you're in reasonably good health, be thankful. It's a gift of grace over which you have little control.

The same is true of family – if you've got a close loving family, you've got a lot to be thankful for. The old saying is, "You can choose your friends, but your family is a given."

I used to listen to a weekly radio program on NPR called, *"A Prairie Home Companion."* The feature of every show was called, *"The News from Lake Wobegon,"* telling of the goings on in the fictitious little town of Lake Wobegon, Minnesota.

In one story, two teenage boys were talking about sex and making babies and what the odds were of being born in Lake Wobegon, as opposed to outer Mongolia. The boys ran through the gambit of religious arguments. Finally, one said to the other, "It's all chance. Life's a big gumball machine. When it's your time to be born, someone comes along and puts a coin in the slot, and down the chute you come. One second, you might come out in Lake Wobegon; a second later, you might come out in Timbuktu."

Sometimes it feels that way, doesn't it? Did you choose your birthday? Your birth order? Your immediate family? Your extended family? All these pieces of your biography are gifts you didn't choose and over which you have little control. Take a moment to be thankful for the family to which you belong. While you're at it, take a moment to be thankful for your friends,

How many friends do you have? When asked, most would say, "five or six." That's true friends, not acquaintances or fair-weather friends. True friends are those who know you, warts and all, and love you just the same!

Friendships don't just happen. They come as a gift – something you don't earn or deserve; but something you receive almost despite yourself.

If friendship is a gift, so is personal devotion and loyalty. A church member once took me on a tour of her company. As we walked through the various departments, she introduced me to her employees. She had something nice to say about each one and how much she appreciated their loyalty and hard work.

The thought came to me: you can hire somebody to do a job and pay them a decent wage. Hopefully, you get what you paid for. But when someone you hire goes the extra mile, you can only be thankful. You can pay for service, but you can't buy loyalty and devotion. This is why, when you go out to eat, the money you leave as a tip is properly called a "gratuity." It's a token of gratitude for the grace you've received.

Our local newspaper, *The Odessa (Texas) American,* where I was serving at the time, took a random survey of people on the street and asked them what they were most thankful for. One respondent said she was most grateful for her relationship to Jesus Christ.

Can you think of a better reason to be thankful? Through the death and resurrection of Jesus Christ our sins are forgiven, and we're reconciled to God by faith in him. It's not something we earn or deserve in any way. Paul said it best in his Letter to the Ephesians:

> "For by grace you have been saved through faith; and this is not your own doing, it is a gift of God ..." (Ephesians 2:8 RSV). John puts it this way: "And from his fullness have we all received, grace upon grace." (*John 1:16 RSV*).

You get the point: There are many reasons to be thankful, and the greatest of them all is God's love sealed once and for all in the death and resurrection of Jesus Christ. In response, I challenge you to be grateful for God's amazing grace and say thank you at some point every day, and if you're willing to stretch your linguistic skills, say it in Spanish, *"Gracias, Señor, por tu gracia."*

Comfort the Afflicted,
Afflict the Comfortable

Acts 19:1-10; 21-41

The title of the sermon comes from a 19th Century journalist named Finley Peter Dunne, a contemporary of Joseph Pulitzer. He writes,

> "Th newspaper does ivrything f'r us. It runs th' polis foorce an' th' banks, commands th' milishy, controls th' ligislachure, baptizes th' young, marries th' foolish, comforts th' afflicted, afflicts th' comfortable, buries th' dead an' roasts thim aftherward." *(1902 October 4, The Province, Mr. Dooley on Newspaper Publicity by F. P. Dunne)*

Preachers were quick to apply Dooley's words to the Christian faith contending that the nature of the gospel is to comfort the afflicted and afflict the comfortable. I like to think that's the job of every Christian, not just preachers - to offer hope and consolation to those who are hurting while standing strong against the evils of injustice and oppression and selfish pursuit.

This is what we find in the scripture lesson for today: Paul offered the Ephesians the promise of salvation through faith in Jesus Christ. In so doing, he denounced the sin of idolatry that was so prevalent in the city of Ephesus.

Paul had wanted to go to Ephesus for a long time. It's easy to understand why. Ephesus was the largest city in Asia Minor and the provincial seat of power for the Roman Empire. It was the home of the great Temple of Artemis, one of the Seven Wonders of the World, measuring twice the size of the Parthenon and serving as both temple and marketplace. People came from far and near to pay homage to Artemis and shop.

In addition to the Temple of Artemis, Ephesus offered baths and brothels, one of the largest libraries in the world, and a 25,000-seat amphitheater for plays and sporting events. What's more, Ephesus was a port city on the Aegean Sea that attracted a steady stream of sailors, merchants, and travelers from all over the world.

When he got to Ephesus, Paul had his work cut out for him – politicians and prostitutes, gofers and gladiators – Ephesus had them all. If he could win them over to Christ, think of how the gospel might spread from there! For three months he went to the synagogue and tried to convince the Jews that Jesus was the Promised Messiah of the Jewish faith. When that failed, he went to the Gentiles. (*Acts 19:8-10*)

After three years, trouble began. Paul spoke out against Artemis and the worship of idols. Theologically, he was on solid ground. The First Commandment clearly states, "Thou shalt have no other gods before me." (*Exodus 20:3-5 RSV*)

Paul's preaching threatened the livelihood of the silversmiths, who made their living casting silver figurines of Artemis to sell as souvenirs and be used in the practice of idol worship.

The spokesman of the silversmiths was a man named Demitrius, and it didn't take him long to get the whole city up in arms. The citizens of Ephesus filled the theater and began to chant, "Great is Artemis of the Ephesians!"

Two of Paul's companions were dragged into the theater and placed on center stage. You can imagine the outcry. Luke says that Paul wanted to go and address the crowd himself, but his friends held him back. It would be like sending a lamb to slaughter.

Before a riot broke out, a local magistrate intervened. He told the crowd they had nothing to worry about and, if they had a complaint, they could take it to court. Otherwise, they should go home, lest they attract the attention of the Roman soldiers. And they did. As for Paul, he quickly said his goodbyes and got on the first ship sailing for Greece. He would never set foot in Ephesus again.

I wonder what Paul was thinking as he sailed from Ephesus to Philippi. Was he filled with regret, or was he satisfied, having had the courage to speak the truth in love? It's worth considering because, to his credit, Paul did a lot of good in Ephesus. For at least two years, the church in Ephesus prospered and grew.

I like to think of Paul as a caring pastor, who practiced what he preached, that he meant it when he said the church was the body of Christ, where "... if one member suffers, all suffer together; and, if one member is honored, all rejoice together." *(1 Corinthians 12:26 RSV)*

I picture Paul as a caring priest, who knew how to comfort the afflicted. But he was also a fiery prophet, who didn't hesitate to afflict the comfortable and challenge the status quo.

This is what he did when he attacked the Temple of Artemis and the worship of idols – He threatened the economic prosperity of the city. It was a gutsy move, and it cost him dearly. In today's world, we'd call it, "political suicide."

I suspect Paul knew the price he would pay for speaking out and taking a stand. I think he would tell us there's a time to comfort the afflicted, and there's time to afflict the comfortable; there's a time to speak words of encouragement and hope to those who are hurting, and there's a time to confront the evils of this world and speak the truth in love, even when it hurts, and even when it costs us dearly.

- This is what Mahatma Ghandi did when he challenged British imperialism and led India in one of the most dramatic revolutions in the history of civilization.
- This is what Nelson Mandela did when he spoke out against apartheid and helped South Africa break the hold of the white minority there.

- This is what Martin Luther King, Jr. did when he marched down the streets of Selma, Alabama and, later, when he spoke on the steps of the Lincoln Memorial and shared his dream of a nation no longer divided by racial segregation.

There's a time to comfort the afflicted, and there's a time to afflict the comfortable. No one knew this better than Harry Emerson Fosdick, one of the pioneers of "the social gospel." In 1922, Fosdick preached a sermon entitled, *"Shall the Fundamentalists Win?"* challenging the fallacies of Biblical fundamentalism. It created a firestorm and cost him his job.

For Fosdick, it was just the beginning. True, he lost his job, but with the help of John D. Rockefeller, he founded Riverside Church near Harlem and began a ministry that reached out to the whole city of New York. It was one of the first churches in the United States – if not the first – to embrace people of every race, religion, and walk of life. He was both friend of the well-to-do and champion of the underdog. Few have made a stronger impact or left a greater legacy of service to their fellow man.

Fosdick wrote a hymn for the opening worship service of Riverside Church on October 5, 1930. The fourth verse of the hymn sums up the challenges we face today and gives voice to our closing prayer:

> "Save us from weak resignation from the evils we deplore. Let the search for thy salvation be our glory evermore. Grant us wisdom, grant us courage, serving Thee whom we adore. Serving Thee whom we adore."

What is that to You?

John 21:1-25

The sovereignty of God to do as he pleases – and for us not to question or complain – can be summarized in these five words: *"What is that to you?"* That's what Jesus asked Peter when Jesus told him that he was to die a martyr's death. He said,

> "'Very truly, I tell you, when you were younger you dressed yourself and went wherever you wanted; but when you are old, you will stretch out your hands, and someone else will dress you and lead you where you do not want to go." Jesus said this to indicate the kind of death by which Peter would glorify God. Then he said to him, 'Follow me.'" (*John 21:18-19 NIV*)

Peter was crucified in Rome in the latter part of the 1st Century A.D. Not only was he crucified, he asked to be hanged upside down because he didn't feel worthy to die in the same manner as the Lord. In prophesying Peter's death, Jesus alluded to how the soldiers would stretch out his arms and tie them over the cross bar, then tie a belt around his waist and lead him to the place where he was to die.

John says, "Peter turned and saw that the disciple whom Jesus loved was following them." When Peter saw him, he asked, "Lord, what about him?" The implication: "Will he also be martyred for your sake?" Jesus answered, "If I want him to remain alive until I return, what is that to you? You must follow me!" (*John 21:20-22 NIV*)

John was the youngest of the disciples and the only one to live to a ripe old age. One tradition has it that, after the crucifixion/resurrection of Jesus, he took Mary, the mother of Jesus, to Ephesus and cared for her there until her death. The *Book of Revelation* begins with letters John wrote to the seven churches of Asia Minor, all situated close to Ephesus. The huge Basilica of St. John in Ephesus was built as a tribute to his place of respect and authority in the early church. And so, here we have two of Jesus' disciples – one, doomed to die a martyr's death; the other, blessed with the prospects of a long and productive life.

Now, be honest: If you'd been Peter, wouldn't you have been just as curious to know the fate of the other disciples? "Lord, what about this man?" It's a fair question, one we'd all like to know. And so, just as Jesus spoke to Peter, he says to us, "What is that to you?"

This is what I hope you'll get out of the sermon today: Whether you feel overly blessed or short-changed, you have a special place in God's family. Jesus died for the forgiven of your sins. If that's the case, don't waste your time comparing your good fortune or misfortune to others, be thankful for the gifts of grace you've received and trust God to give you all you need for a full and abundant life. To help you do this, here are three rules-of-thumb to keep in mind: Rule Number One: *Life isn't fair.* It never has been, it never will be.

When our kids were little, they were quick to complain, "But that's not fair!" The oldest often complained that we were expecting too much out of him. The youngest usually complained that his older brothers got to do things he didn't get to do: The middle child felt overlooked. Looking back, so many of their complaints had to do with fairness, or the lack thereof – one getting a better shake than the other – a little more ice cream or less household chores. To be honest, I suspect much of the conflict in marriage has to do with comparing one with the other.

This leads me to wonder how much conflict in the workplace – and society, in general – stems from comparing one to the other: "Why does he get to come in late, and I have to be here to open the doors? Why is she paid more than me when I'm the one who does all the work?" The list goes on and on. Comparing leads to jealousy, and jealousy leads to resentment and anger.

Let's face it: Life isn't fair, and the more you base your happiness on how you compare with others, the unhappier you're likely to be. Peter was destined to die a martyr's death, while John was destined to live a long and productive life. Don't judge one by the other.

Rule Number Two: *Things are not always as they seem.* What appears to be a blessing may be a curse; what appears to be a curse may turn out to be a blessing in disguise. Perhaps you've heard this little Chinese parable before. It bears repeating:

> "Once there lived a young man on the northern frontier of China. One day, for no reason, his horse bolted and ran away across the border. Despondent, everyone tried to console him, but his father said, "You never know, it could be a blessing." Months later his horse returned bringing with it a splendid stallion. Everyone rejoiced at his good fortune, but his father said, "You never know, it could be a curse." One day the young man went out for a ride and the horse threw him, breaking his leg. Despondent, everyone tried to console him, but his father said, "You never know, it could be a blessing." Sure enough, within weeks nomads crossed the border in battle. Every able-bodied young man took up his bow to defend their village. The casualties were high. Only because of his broken leg was the young man spared. Truly, blessing turns to disaster, and disaster to blessing: The changes have no end, nor can the mystery be fathomed." (*A story by Liu An*)

It's a recurring theme – someone wins the lottery and suddenly has more money than he knows what to do with, but instead of changing his life for the better, it wrecks his life with worry and greed. You get a big promotion at work, but your new job is stressful and time-consuming, and it takes you away from your family. You work and slave to get the house of your dreams only to be weighed down by the burden of monthly payments you can't afford.

Things are not always as they seem. This works both ways. What, at first, seems to be a curse turns out to be an unexpected blessing. That's the essence of this creed found in the Center for Rehabilitation Medicine in New York City:

> "I asked God for strength, that I might achieve; I was made weak, that I might learn humbly to obey; I asked for health, that I might do greater things, I was given infirmity, that I might do better things; I asked for riches, that I might be happy, I was given poverty, that I might be wise; I asked for power, that I might have the praise of others, I was given weakness, that I might feel the need of God; I asked for all things, that I might enjoy life, I was given life, that I might enjoy all things; I got nothing that I asked for but everything that I had hoped for; Almost despite myself, my unspoken prayers were answered, And I am, of all people, most richly blessed."

Things are not always as they seem. That's Rule Number Two. Rule Number Three: *It's not for us to question or judge.*

In the Bible, the person who heads the list of those who questioned the fairness of God's mercy is Job. You know the story: Job was healthy, wealthy, and wise when the rug was pulled out from under him. His health broke, his crops failed, his livestock died, his children got blown away by a tornado. When the dust settled, all he had left was a nagging wife who told him that he'd be better off dead. She asked, "Do you still hold fast your integrity? Curse God and die." *(Job 2:9 RSV)*

Job had every reason to question God's mercy, and he did so with a passion, but it didn't do him any good. After he'd exhausted every complaint, God appeared to him in a whirlwind and asked,

"Where were you when I laid the foundation of the earth? Tell me if you have understanding. Who determined its measurements--surely you know! Or who stretched the line upon it? On what were its bases sunk, or who laid its cornerstone when the morning stars sang together, and all the heavenly beings shouted for joy?" (*Job 38:4-7 RSV*)

God went on to remind Job of the scope of creation, from the great expanse of earth and sky and sea to the infinite detail of birds and fish and animals. Then God asked, "Shall a faultfinder contend with the Almighty?" (*Job 40:2 RSV*) In humility, Job answered,

"I know that you can do all things, and that no purpose of yours can be thwarted ... I have uttered what I did not understand, things too wonderful for me, which I did not know." (*Job 42:2-3 RSV*)

By the end of the book, Job comes to true faith, a faith not based on good fortune – or shaken by tragedy – but anchored in the steadfast love of the Lord, both in the good times and the bad. The upshot of it all is this: It's not for us to question or complain but rather to be content with what we have. Paul told Timothy:

"There is great gain in godliness with contentment; for we brought nothing into the world, and we can take nothing out of the world; but if we have food and clothing, with these we shall be content." (*1 Timothy 6:6-8 RSV*)

Let's be honest: We're all prone to wanting a bigger house or a better car or some new gadget or toy, while the truth is most of us have more than we need. Despite what others say, the grass on the other side of the fence may not be as green as it seems; and, seen from the other side, the grass on our side of the fence is plenty green enough. The bottom line is this: Be content with what you have, and be thankful, both in plenty and in want. One of my favorite prayers is the Covenant Prayer of John Wesley. It goes like this:

> "I am no longer my own, but thine. Put me to what thou wilt, rank me with whom thou wilt. Put me to doing, put me to suffering. Let me be employed for thee or laid aside for thee, exalted for thee or brought low for thee. Let me be full, let me be empty. Let me have all things, let me have nothing. I freely and heartily yield all things to thy pleasure and disposal."

Trust God to give you all you need for a full and abundant life and know this: The kingdom of God lies ahead, not behind. Instead of looking over your shoulder and comparing your lot in life with others, remember the words of Helen Limmel, who wrote,

> "Turn your eyes upon Jesus, look full in His wonderful face, and the things of earth will grow strangely dim, in the light of His glory and grace."

Remember Zebulun and Naphtali!

Isaiah 9:1-4; Matthew 4:12-17

Are you a name dropper? Do you like to impress your friends with people you've met, places you've been? Next time you're in a group and someone talks about what a mess our world is in, simply say, "If you think things are bad today, just remember Zebulun and Naphtali!"

Here's the big picture: Zebulun and Naphtali were regions in northern Palestine just west of the Sea of Galilee. The names refer to sons of Jacob and two of the twelve tribes of Israel. They're important because they link Isaiah's prophecy of the coming of the Messiah with Matthew's account of the inauguration of Jesus' ministry.

It goes back to the 8th century B.C. Northern Palestine, aka, Israel, refused to pay taxes to Assyria, the powerhouse of the region, and the Assyrians retaliated, destroying the capital city of Samaria and deporting the Jews. Isaiah says,

"God brought into contempt the land of Zebulun and Naphtali." Yet, he goes on to say, "Nevertheless, there will be no more gloom for those who were in distress ... In the past he humbled the land of Zebulun and Naphtali, but in the future he will honor Galilee of the nations, by the Way of the Sea, beyond the Jordan – the people walking in darkness have seen a great light; on those living in the land of deep darkness a light has dawned." (*Isaiah 9:1-2 NIV*)

Just as Isaiah predicted, the exile came to an end. Jewish immigrants began moving back and settling in, reclaiming what was left of the vacant fields including home sites, wells, and villages.

One tiny village was Nazareth, where Jesus grew up. Not only was Isaiah's prophecy fulfilled, Zebulun and Naphtali came to demonstrate how God can bring new life from that which seems to be dead and buried.

The Cunningham home in Wichita Falls, Texas, was a large, two-story colonial mansion sitting on a 5-acre tract of land in the west part of town. After the owners died, the house sat vacant for years. It was badly dilapidated and in need of repair when, in 1989, the survivors gave the property to the local hospice organization. Volunteers of Hospice of Wichita Falls went to work and spent hundreds of man-hours to renovate. Donations poured in. The house was refurbished inside and out. In no time, it was as good as new.

The Hospice staff moved in and went to work. I dropped by one day and stood there in the entranceway. The phones were ringing. Nurses and volunteers were busy coming and going. The place was a beehive of activity. As I looked at the elegant staircase spiraling up to the second floor, I couldn't help but think how proud Shem Cunningham would have been – and how amazed – to see his old home place teeming with new vitality and life.

It made me think of this recurring theme of the Bible, that out of what seems to be dead, God brings new life into being. To the barren old womb of Sarah, God gave a child (Genesis17), in the dry, parched wilderness of the Sinai, God caused streams of living water to flow (Isaiah43), from the stump of Jesse, God raised up the shoot of David (Isaiah 11:1-10), from the darkness of Galilee, God brought forth the light of the world, Jesus Christ.

You see where this is going: In the face of despair, when the bottom falls out from under you, when all seems hopeless and lost, remember Zebulun and Naphtali. Let the memory of what God did for his people so long ago in Galilee be a source of hope for you today. The Good News is, God can turn your darkest night into day.

Have hope. In the meantime, be patient. The fullness of God's appearing comes about in God's own good time. This is yet another great theme of the Bible: The promise of deliverance is not necessarily immediate. The children of Israel suffered as slaves in Egypt for four hundred years before God sent Moses to set them free. They wandered in the desert for forty years before reaching the Promised Land. They spent seventy years in exile in Babylon before God brought them back to the land of Judah.

It's a bitter pill to swallow, to have to wait on the Lord because we are, by nature, impatient. We want what we want when we want it. We live in a world of instant gratification, and we don't like to be put on hold. We can all identify with the little placard that reads, "Lord, give me patience, and I mean right now!"

God doesn't step to our pace. If we're to experience the fullness of God's blessings, we must learn to move in rhythm with God's Spirit, not bolting ahead, but holding back, waiting for God to take the lead. A passage in the *Book of Lamentations* reads,

> "The steadfast love of the Lord never ceases, his mercies never come to an end; they are new every morning; great is Thy faithfulness. The Lord is my portion, says my soul, therefore, I will hope in him. The Lord is good to those who wait for him, to the soul that seeks him. It is good that one should wait quietly for the salvation of the Lord ... For the Lord will not cast off forever. Although he causes grief, he will have compassion according to the abundance of his steadfast love, for he does not willingly afflict or grieve anyone." (*Lamentations 3:22-26; 31-33 RSV*)

Several years ago, I took a tour of the missions in San Antonio. As you may know, there are the remains of five Spanish missions there, the most famous being the Alamo. As the tour guide explained the long and laborious process of how these missions were established, it dawned on me that the founding priest never lived to see the completion of his mission. In each case, there was a succession of priests who spent the better part of their lives overseeing the construction of just one phase of the total project – the basilica, the infirmary, the school, the living quarters, the aqueducts, the outer wall. One generation followed another as faithful men and women did their part and passed on.

Be patient. Remember that, in the words of the psalmist, "... For a thousand years in your sight are like yesterday when it is past, or like a watch in the night." (*Psalms 90:4 RSV*)

Galilee was dark for six hundred years before the light of God's revelation began to shine once more. The next time you find yourself in a tizzy because you don't seem to be getting anywhere or making any progress, when everything seems to be moving at glacier speed, remember Zebulun and Naphtali! Worthwhile goals take time to achieve. Be patient. Rest assured that, in time, God will come through. He always has. He always will. Have hope. Be patient, and as you wait for God to take the lead, be persevering.

As many of you know, I enjoy sailing. I used to have a small sailboat on Lake Brownwood. I'd go there on days off to get away from it all. Learning to sail, you not only learn the basic skills and techniques of sailing but the language of sailing as well – the names of all the sheets and halyards and cleats and stays. Plus, you learn to appreciate old expressions like, "Batten down the hatches, mateys," and "Helms alee."

One of the sailing expressions I like best is the admonition, "stay the course." In olden days, a storm would come up at sea, and the ship would start to take a beating. The crew would be tempted to abandon the mission and head for the nearest port, but the captain would order, "Nay, stay the course!" Stay on the present heading. Weather the storm. Have confidence. This, too, shall pass. Stay the course. It's a useful expression, not only at sea or out on the lake, but in everyday life as well.

Before joining the PC(USA), I served as a United Methodist pastor. One of my first appointments was to a little country church about ten miles east of Denton, Texas called Oak Grove United Methodist Church. The Oak Grove church began in 1878 and, in its heyday, boasted a congregation of over one hundred members. For years it was the church of choice for farming families in the area and, whenever there was a death in the community, the folks would come from all over to gather at the little cemetery out back. Over the years, as society became less agrarian and the kids went off to college and settled in the cities, the population dwindled, and the Oak Grove church declined. As religious views shifted and mainline denominations fell out of favor, long-time members defected, and the membership got even smaller. As rising costs met head-to-head with limited resources and the folks at Oak Grove could no longer pay a minister, the majority felt that it was time to call it quits.

Two members of Oak Grove took exception. They were an older couple and long-time members of Oak Grove. The wife was the pianist, her husband, the self-appointed custodian of the property. In the wintertime, he'd come to the church in the wee hours of the morning to light the space heater so the church would be warm when the others got there.

As what few remaining members fell away, this older couple continued to come on Sunday mornings. They'd sit on a pew together and take turns reading the Sunday School lesson. They'd hold hands and pray, ending with the Lord's Prayer. Sometimes they'd sing the Doxology. Then they'd go home. Though they were now a congregation of only two, they were determined to keep the doors opened for as long as they were able. Weeks and months went by, and they held fast. They seldom missed a Sunday. Then, one Sunday, another couple joined them. Then another and another. By the time we arrived in 1972, they had a solid core of eleven members. As you might guess, it's grown considerably since, so that Oak Grove is a strong and vibrant church today with every prospect for continued growth and prosperity.

I've often thought about this old couple sitting there in that little Oak Grove church on Sunday mornings. To this day, they're an inspiration that says to me when the tide turns and you find yourself in the minority, when you start to get discouraged and want to throw in the towel, stay the course. Keep the faith. In time, God will prove his faithfulness.

No one knew this better than the poet, Katharina von Schlegel, who, in the early 18th Century, penned the words to the hymn,

"Be still my soul, the Lord is on thy side; bear patiently the cross of grief or pain; leave to thy God to order and provide; in every change he faithful will remain. Be still, my soul, thy best, thy heavenly friend through thorny ways leads to a joyful end." *(UMC Hymnal, p. 534)*

O.K., let's see how well you've been listening. Next time you feel down in the dumps, that all is lost, that it's all over but the crying, what are you going to say to yourself? (Don't be afraid to shout) *REMEMBER ZEBULUN AND NAPHTALI!* Next time you feel like you're getting nowhere fast, that you're stuck on high center and the world is passing you by, what are you going to say? (Altogether now) *REMEMBER ZEBULUN AND NAPHTALI!* Next time you get discouraged and wonder, what's the use? What's your battle cry going to be? *REMEMBER ZEBULUN AND NAPHTALI!*

Remember Zebulun and Naphtali! Never forget that out of the darkness of Zebulun and Naphtali came the light of the world, Jesus Christ.

When Does Easter Come?

John 20:1-18

The title of the sermon this morning is inspired by an article entitled, "When is Easter is this year?" *(Christianity Today, April 20, 2000)*

It's a good question. Easter never falls on the same date, year after year. It can come as early as March 22 and as late as April 25. So, how is the date is determined? In 325 A.D. the Council of Nicea came up with "The Easter Rule." According to the bishops, Easter falls on the first Sunday after the first full moon after the vernal equinox. Aren't you glad you came to church this morning?

In the sermon this morning, I'd like to rephrase the question and simply ask, *"When does Easter come?"* What I want to know is this: When did the power of Jesus' resurrection come to Mary Magdalene, Peter and John, and the other disciples in the gospel lesson for today? Once we answer this question, we can go on to ask when will the reality of Jesus' resurrection come to us and to those we love? The story begins,

> "Early on the first day of the week, while it was still dark, Mary Magdalene came to the tomb and saw that the stone had been removed from the tomb. So, she ran and went to Simon Peter and the other disciple, the one whom Jesus loved, and said to them, 'They have taken the Lord out of the tomb, and we do not know where they have laid him.'" *(John 20:1-2 RSV)*

According to John, Mary sees the empty tomb, recognizes that the body of Jesus is not there, but, in no way, concludes that he has been raised from the dead. He's missing, that's all. Easter has not come for Mary. Not yet.

This is our first hint as to how to answer the question, "When does Easter come?" It does not come when we gather enough empirical evidence.

The empty tomb alone is not proof of the resurrection. That's frustrating because we are rational men and women who are open to reason and willing to accept the results of quantifiable data. We're students of the scientific method: Develop a hypothesis, test it over and over in a controlled environment and trust the outcome to be factual and true.

This has led us to put our hopes in such discoveries as the Shroud of Turin – the ancient linen believed to be the burial cloth in which Jesus' body was wrapped, – and the Dead Sea Scrolls – scriptures and writings of the Essenes found near the Dead Sea. If only we could nail it down, gather enough tangible evidence to document the historical record, then we could prove, once and for all, that Jesus was the Messiah, the Son of God, who rose from the dead that we might have the promise of eternal life. If only the empty tomb were enough. But it's not. Easter comes by faith, and faith alone.

When we were first introduced to algebra in high school, we learned a theorem called, *"The Transitive Law of Property."* It went like this: *"If A is greater than B and B is greater than C, then A is greater than C."* You can imagine the possibilities. Using the Transitive Law of Property, you can prove all sorts of things. One, not in the textbook, is this: Peanuts are better than ice cream. How so? Peanuts are better than nothing, and nothing's better than ice cream!

Sounds logical, only it's not necessarily true. Whether peanuts are better than ice cream is a matter of personal taste. Mary Magdalene saw the empty tomb, but it didn't prove a thing, and it certainly didn't transform her life. Easter, for her, was yet to come.

As the story goes, Mary ran to tell Peter and John, and they raced to the tomb to see for themselves. Sure enough, the stone had been rolled away and the body was missing, just as she'd said. I can imagine how they must have stood there scratching their heads, wondering what had happened. John says, "for as yet they did not understand the scripture, that he must rise from the dead. Then the disciples returned to their homes." (*John 20:9-10 RSV*) John goes on to say,

> "But Mary stood weeping outside the tomb. As she wept, she bent over to look into the tomb; and she saw two angels in white, sitting where the body of Jesus had been lying, one at the head and the other at the feet. They said to her, 'Woman, why are you weeping?' She said to them, 'They have taken away my Lord, and I do not know where they have laid him.' When she had said this, she turned around and saw Jesus standing there, but she did not know that it was Jesus." (John 20:11-14 RSV)

You'd think that the witness of others would be enough to inspire faith in the resurrection of Jesus, especially the witness of a couple of angels. In Luke's account of the resurrection, the angels not only appeared to Mary, but they asked her, "Why do you seek the living among the dead? He is not here but he has risen. Remember how he told you, while he was in Galilee, that the Son of Man must be handed over to sinners, and be crucified, and on the third day rise again?" (*Luke 24:5-7 RSV*)

Still, Mary is unconvinced. She has yet to experience the power of Jesus' resurrection.

This is our second hint as to how to answer the question, "When does Easter come?" It does not come when we gather enough witnesses. The faith of our fathers and mothers and neighbors and friends is important, but it's not enough to transform us into the image of Christ. For that, we need to see and hear and experience the risen Christ for ourselves.

Some like to say, "God has many children, but no grandchildren." That is to say, the church of Jesus Christ is made up of first-generation believers, each coming to faith in his or her own way, each being born again in the spirit of the living Christ. In other words, it's up to you and me to experience a first-person relationship with Jesus Christ, not just know about him through others.

In his book, *When Bad Things Happen to Good People,* Rabbi Harold Kushner talks about the importance of the community of faith. He tells the story of Harry Golden, who once asked his father, "If you don't believe in God, why do go to synagogue so regularly? His father said, "Jews go to synagogue for all sorts of reasons. My friend Garfinkle, who is Orthodox, goes to talk with God. I go to talk to Garfinkle." *"When Bad Things Happen to Good People," p. 122)*

There's nothing wrong with going to church to talk to each other. Christian fellowship lies at the heart of a life of faith. But fellowship alone is not enough. Salvation doesn't come vicariously, one gleaning from the experience of others. It comes by personal encounter with the living Christ. This is what happened to Mary. According to John, Mary turned and saw what she took to be the gardener standing behind her. He asked, "Why are you weeping? Whom do you seek?" Still not having experienced the resurrection, she said, "Sir, if you have carried him away, tell me where you have laid him, and I will take him away." At that moment, Jesus said, "Mary!" and Mary exclaimed, "Rabboni," (which means teacher). *(John 20:13-15 RSV)*

This leads to the answer to our question, "When does Easter come?" Easter comes when the Lord calls your name, and you hear his voice, and you respond in faith and devotion and love.

The Bible is filled with stories of those who did just that. Take Abraham, for example. God picked Abraham to be the father of his chosen people, Israel. When Abraham heard God's voice, he packed up his family and journeyed into the land of Canaan. (Genesis 12:1-3)

Then there's Moses. God called Moses from a burning bush and sent him down into Egypt to tell the Pharaoh, "Let my people go." (Exodus 3)

And let's not forget Samuel. Samuel was only a child when God called his name, and he answered, "Speak, Lord, for thy servant hears." *(1 Samuel 3:7-11 RSV)*

Our list goes on to include Peter, Andrew, James, and John, to whom Jesus said, "Follow me, and I will make you fishers of men." *(Matthew 4:19 RSV)* It also includes the other disciples, men like Matthew the tax collector, who walked away from a lucrative position of prominence and power to follow Jesus.

Finally, there's the Apostle Paul, who met Jesus in a flash of blinding light on the Damascus Road. (Acts 9:1-9) The common denominator in each story is this: God calls, and those whom he calls hear his voice and respond in faith.

This is what happened to Mary. Jesus called her by name, and her eyes were opened, and she recognized that this "gardener" was Jesus, the risen Christ. At that moment, Easter came to Mary. The power of Christ's resurrection from the dead, the forgiveness of sins, and the hope of eternal life were hers, never to be taken away.

When does Easter come? Easter comes when God calls your name, and you hear his voice, and you respond in faith. The question is, has God called your name? Have you heard God's voice? Have you responded in faith? *Has Easter come for you?*

Don't be ashamed to confess, "No. Not yet." Truth to tell, not everyone has heard the voice of God, not everyone has been transformed in the likeness of Jesus Christ. If God has spoken to you, rejoice and be glad. Walk in faith. If you have not heard the voice of God calling your name, don't despair. There may be a simple explanation. Perhaps it's because you're not listening. You're too busy, preoccupied with more pressing matters. Or it could be that you're dubious, not sure you can trust such an intangible reality as the voice of God. Yet another reason you've not heard your name called might be just that – God hasn't called your name. Have you ever considered this possibility?

I trust you're familiar with the video series, *"The Chosen,"* about Jesus and the disciples? If not, I highly recommend it. Kathy and I recently began watching it again for the third time. It's that good. We were watching an episode the other night when the thought struck me: Of all the people Jesus met on the streets of Galilee, he only chose twelve men to be his disciples. That's not to say he rejected the others, only that they didn't suit his purposes at the time.

This inspired me to think: Perhaps those not chosen are like the players warming the bench at a football, basketball, or baseball game, players that are in top shape, fully aware of what to do when the coach calls their name, ready to take the field and do their part at any moment.

Granted, you won't find this explanation in the Bible, but the more I think about it, the more it appeals to me. It emphasizes the importance of the team, not the individual. It focuses on the coach who calls the shots, not the players waiting their turn to play. It leaves open the possibility that, in God's time, you may be the next to be called. If so, will you be ready?

If this speaks to you, try this: As you wait for God to call your name, stay fit, study your Bible, pray without ceasing. Be patient. Have confidence that, in time, the very same God who breathed into your nostrils the breath of life may one day call your name, and on that day, Easter will come to you, and, if you're willing to offer little Samuel's prayer: "Speak, Lord, for thy servant hears," you will be born again to new life in Jesus' name.

Christ and Adam

1 Corinthians 15:22

Are you a major league baseball fan? When our boys were growing up, we used to watch the playoff games and the World Series on TV. Funny, while I don't remember much about the players, I will never forget watching the guy sitting in the stands behind home plate. He was hard to miss. I'm guessing the camera man was shooting from a platform just behind center field. This gave the viewer a clear view of the action: The pitcher on the mound, the batter off to one side of the plate, the umpire leaning in over the catcher and, in the distance, this non-descript fan sitting in the bleachers a few rows up, holding up a sign for all to see: *"John 3:16."* No matter what teams were playing, he'd be there to offer his personal testimony to the world: "For God so loved the world that he gave his only begotten Son, that whosoever believeth in him should not perish, but have eternal life." I often wondered who he was and what compelled him to want to save lost sinners from their fallen state in this way.

I lost track of him over the years, and I miss him. Thinking of him pricks my conscience and leads me to ask: if I were sitting in the bleachers holding up a sign, what would it say? What one verse of scripture would I choose over all the others? *What verse would you choose?*

For what it's worth, my sign would read, *"1ˢᵗ Corinthians 15:22."* I admit it's not as catchy as John 3:16, but it's every bit as important: "As in Adam all die, so also in Christ shall all be made alive" (*1 Corinthians 15:22* (RSV)

Why is this verse so important? Because it sums up the biblical drama of sin and salvation: The same God who created Adam – that sinful, rebellious father of the human race – also sent his only begotten son, Jesus, who knew no sin, to open the gates of heaven for all who put their faith in him: "As in Adam all die, so also in Christ shall all be made alive."

We commonly refer to the story of Adam and Eve in the Garden of Eden (*Genesis 3*) as the source of our "original sin," not that our sinfulness is all that original, but that it stems from the origin: It's in our genes. To put it simply, their story is our story:

- We are those beloved children of God who are created in God's image and endowed with God's Spirit and placed in the wonderland of God's creation.
- We are those beloved children who refuse to submit to God's authority over our lives.
- We are those beloved children who insist on doing our own thing, in our own way, on our own time and, in the process, making life difficult for ourselves and others.

Like Adam and Eve, we're rotten to the core, and there's nothing we can do to overcome it. John Calvin called this, "the depravity of man." He writes: "So depraved is (our) nature, that we can be moved or impelled only to evil ..." *(The Institutes of the Christian Religion, pp.294-295).*

When I was growing up, I was taught that we were born into a state of innocence and were counted as sinful only when we reached the age of accountability, which roughly corresponds to the onset of puberty. Now we know better. Studies show that children – even infants – are just as egocentric and prone to sin as the rest of us. From earliest childhood, they exhibit the same selfish tendencies as their parents. Oh, you could say they might be innocent the first time they take a cookie out of the cookie jar after being told not to, but you'd better believe the next time, they know exactly what they're doing. If there is an age of innocence, it's short-lived. Paul said it best when he told the Romans: "None is righteous; no, not one." (*Romans 3:10 RSV*).

So, if the bad news is, "as in Adam all die," the Good News is, "so also in Christ shall all be made alive." To go back to the World Series, it's a whole new ball game! Just as the Old Creation started with Adam, the New Creation started with Jesus Christ. As Paul told the Corinthians:

> "… If anyone is in Christ, he is a new creation; the old has passed away, behold, the new has come. All this is from God, who through Christ reconciled us to himself and gave us the ministry of reconciliation; that is, God was in Christ reconciling the world to himself, not counting their trespasses against them, and entrusting to us the message of reconciliation." (*2 Corinthians 5:17-19 (RSV*).

Here's the key to connecting the dots: Just as we had nothing to do with the fall of Adam, neither can we take credit for this New Creation God has established in Jesus Christ. We're just as sinful as ever. The difference is that God has chosen to count us as righteous, even though we're not. This is the way Paul puts it in his Letter to the Romans: "God proves his love for us in that while we still were sinners Christ died for us" (*Romans 5:8 RSV*).

As incredible as it seems, God has acted, once and for all, to reconcile the world to himself through the death and resurrection of Jesus Christ. Despite our sinful nature, God chooses to love us unconditionally. The question is how are we to respond to such love as this? We can be skeptical and unbelieving, or we can be trusting and grateful, accepting God's gracious gift of forgiveness, while forgiving and loving others in return.

Many years ago, the calendar we used to mark our days changed from "B.C." to "A.D." A new era of history began. Ever since, this new era has been known to people of faith as *"Anno Domini,"* the year of our Lord.

Knowing this, Let this mark a new beginning in your life. A New Creation of grace and forgiveness began with the atoning the death and resurrection of Jesus Christ. Dare to leave your old life of doubt and fear at the foot of the Cross. Dare to accept the gift of God's grace and love. Believe the Gospel: "As in Adam all die, so also in Christ shall all be made alive."

A Funeral Message from the Book of Ecclesiastes

Having just heard these comforting words of scripture, "The Lord is my Shepherd, I shall not want," (*Psalm 23:1 RSV*) and Jesus' promise, "… where I am, there you will be also …" (*John 14:3 RSV*), I'd like to share a few verses from the Book of Ecclesiastes. It begins,

"Meaningless! Meaningless! says the Teacher. Utterly meaningless! What do people gain from all their labors at which they toil under the sun? Generations come and generations go, but the earth remains forever. The sun rises and the sun sets, and hurries back to where it rises. The wind blows to the south and turns to the north, round and round it goes, ever returning on its course. All streams flow into the sea, yet the sea is never full. To the place the streams come from, there they return again. All things are wearisome, more than one can say. The eye never has enough of seeing, nor the ear its fill of hearing. What has been will be again, what has been done will be done again; there is nothing new under the sun. It was here already, long ago; it was here before our time. No one remembers the former generations, and even those yet to come will not be remembered by those who follow them." (*Ecclesiastes 1:2-11 NIV*)

I admit, The *Book of Ecclesiastes* sounds cynical and depressing. According to Ecclesiastes everything about this mortal life falls short of our expectations and is destined to die.

- As for wisdom, Ecclesiastes says, "For with much wisdom comes much sorrow; the more knowledge, the more grief." (*Ecclesiastes 1:18 NIV*)
- As for pleasure, Ecclesiastes says, "Laughter, I said, is madness. And what does pleasure accomplish?" (*Ecclesiastes 2:2 NIV*) Truth to tell, all forms of pleasure and entertainment are short-lived. Like a video arcade, you put a token in the slot, enjoy a couple of moments of exhilaration, and the game is over.
- As for achievements, Ecclesiastes says, "... great houses, vineyards, servants, herds, and flocks ... when I surveyed all that my hands had done and what I had toiled to achieve, everything was meaningless, a chasing after the wind." (*Ecclesiastes 2:4-11 paraphrased*). It's true. Think of sandcastles on the beach. No matter how elaborate and time consuming, they are soon to be washed away by the rising tide.
- As for justice, Ecclesiastes says, "... a person may labor with wisdom, knowledge, and skill, and then leave all he owns to one who has not toiled for it. This too is meaningless, a chasing after the wind." (*Ecclesiastes 2:21-23 NIV*)

Life is a vicious cycle: "Everyone comes naked from their mother's womb, and as everyone comes, so they depart. They take nothing from their toil that they can carry in their hands.

This too is a grievous evil. As everyone comes, so they depart, and what do they gain, since they toil for the wind?" (*Ecclesiastes 5:15-16 NIV*)

If Ecclesiastes is telling it like it is, what are you going to do? If everything about this mortal life is meaningless and short-lived, where are you going to turn? There is but one answer: Turn to God. God alone is sovereign over all creation. As scripture says, "The eternal God is your refuge, and underneath are the everlasting arms." (*Deuteronomy 33:27 NIV*) While all else is destined to fade away; only God is eternal, steadfast, and true. Isaiah writes,

"The grass withers, the flowers fade, but the Word of God endures forever." (*Isaiah 40:8 NIV*)

Just don't stop there. The Good News is, "God so loved the world that he gave his only begotten Son, that whoever believes in him should not perish, but have eternal life." (*John 3:16 RSV*)

Jesus died on the Cross and rose from the dead to set us free from the vanity of this fallen world and to give us the promise of life everlasting. As Paul put it, "God proves his love for us in that, while we were yet sinners, Christ died for us." (*Romans 5:8 RSV*)

Paul echoes the words of Ecclesiastes when he tells the Corinthians,

> "If only for this life we have hope in Christ, we are of all people most to be pitied. But Christ has indeed been raised from the dead, the first fruits of those who have fallen asleep." (1 Corinthians 15:19-20 RSV) Unlike the fickle, elusive nature of the world in which we live, "Jesus Christ is the same, yesterday, today and forever." (*Hebrews 13:8 RSV*)

The bottom line is this: The secular life this world has to offer, with its endless attractions and temptations, is ultimately meaningless – a mere chasing after the wind. By contrast, if you live by faith and walk in the footsteps of Jesus, you will find opportunities for peace, joy, and love wherever you are, as long as you live. In the words of an old gospel song,

> "Turn your eyes upon Jesus; look full in his wonderful face, and the things of earth will grow strangely dim in the light of his glory and grace." (Helen Lemmel)

That's the essence of the sermon for today. In closing, it's only fitting for Ecclesiastes to have the final word. It's found in the last chapter. It reads like a hymn of triumph starting with an admonition and ending with a blessing. It goes like this:

> "Remember your Creator in the days of your youth, before the days of trouble come and the years approach when you will say, "I find no pleasure in them"—before the sun and the light and the moon and the stars grow dark, and the clouds return after the rain; when the keepers of the house tremble, and the strong men stoop, when the grinders cease because they are few, and those looking through the windows grow dim; when the doors to the street are closed and the sound of grinding fades; when people rise up at the sound of birds, but all their songs grow faint; when people are afraid of heights and of dangers in the streets; when the almond tree blossoms and the grasshopper drags itself along, and desire no longer is stirred. Then people go to their eternal home and mourners go about the streets. Remember him—before the silver cord is severed, and the golden bowl is broken; before the pitcher is shattered at the spring, and the wheel broken at the well, and the dust returns to the ground from which it came, and the spirit returns to God who gave it." (*Ecclesiastes 12:1-7 NIV*)

A Glorified Body

I'd like to introduce you to one of the most important and difficult concepts of the New Testament – the glorified body of Jesus. You've already caught a glimpse of it:

- When Jesus appeared to Mary at the empty tomb, she thought he was the gardener.
- When Jesus appeared to the disciples in the Upper Room, somehow, he came through the locked door. (*John 20:14-15*)
- When he came back a week later for Thomas' benefit, again the door was locked, yet he came in and showed Thomas his nail-scarred hands and feet. (*John 20:24-29*)
- Two of his followers were on their way home to Emmaus when he appeared, talked with them at length about his passion, death, and resurrection, but they had no idea that it was he. They compelled him to come to their home and eat with them and, as he broke bread with them, their eyes were opened, and they recognized it was he. Then, just like that, he disappeared. (*Luke 24:13-32*) How do you explain that? And what difference does it make for us today?

We often recite The Apostles Creed and affirm, "I believe in … the resurrection of the body and the life everlasting." What do we mean by that? Will we be raised from the dead like Jesus? Will we inherit a glorified body when we die? We need to come clean on these things because, if you didn't already know it, there's a lot of misinformation floating around about the resurrection and the afterlife.

I conducted my first funeral in 1971. I was student pastor of the Prosper United Methodist Church, north of Dallas. The funeral took place in McKinney, Texas; the burial was in a country cemetery near Prosper. I rode out to the cemetery with the funeral director. As we turned into the cemetery heading north, he made a point to tell me that the head of the body would be placed to the left of the family. "What difference does that make?" I asked. He looked at me with furrowed eyebrows and said, "Because that's where you're supposed to stand." "Oh," I said. "I didn't know that." He said, "And I bet you didn't know that the graves are laid out east and west, did you?" I looked at the gravestones we were passing. Sure enough, they were all lined up in neat, orderly rows, perpendicular to the entrance. "Why is that?" I asked. Like an exasperated professor, he said, "So that the bodies can rise up to greet the Son of Man when he appears in the east at the Second Coming." Honestly, the thought had never occurred to me. After the burial, I looked down at the grave and tried to imagine how this man's corpse, now sealed in the casket, was going to sit up and welcome Jesus as he appeared in the clouds. I wondered to myself that day: Is this what we mean by the resurrection of the body? Surely, there's more to it than that. But what?

The resurrection appearances of Jesus give us a clue. His glorified body is both physical and spiritual. The disciples were able to recognize him and talk with him, yet he was not bound by time and space. How can we put this in terms we can understand? Paul uses an analogy. He told the Corinthians:

> "Some will ask, 'How are the dead raised? With what kind of body will they come?' How foolish! What you sow does not come to life unless it dies. When you sow, you do not plant the body that will be, but just a seed, perhaps of wheat or of something else. But God gives it a body as he has determined, and to each

kind of seed he gives its own body." (*1 Corinthians (15:35-38 NIV*)

Paul says, "So it is with the resurrection of the dead. What is sown is perishable, what is raised is imperishable ... it is sown a physical body, it is raised a spiritual body." (*1 Corinthians 15:42-44*) He admits it's a mystery, yet he goes on to say: "We shall not all sleep, but we shall all be changed, in the moment, in the twinkling of an eye, at the last trumpet ... the dead will be raised imperishable, and we will be changed. For the perishable must clothe itself with the imperishable, and the mortal with immortality. When (this happens) ... then the saying that is written will come true: 'Death has been swallowed up in victory. Where, O death, is your victory? Where, O death, is your sting?' The sting of death is sin, but thanks be to God who gives us the victory in Christ Jesus our Lord" (*1 Corinthians 15:52-57 NIV*).

What does this mean for us today? First, it means that this mortal body we live in is only a shell. It's not meant to last forever. Nor is it meant to be resuscitated at some future point in time. It's only a temporary dwelling. Our permanent dwelling is yet to come. Paul says:

"For we know that if this earthly tent we live in is destroyed, we have a building from God, not built by human hands, eternal in the heavens." (*2 Corinthians 5:1 NIV*)

In his children's book, *The Fall of Freddie the Leaf,* Leo Buscaglia tells the plight of a beautiful leaf who held on to his branch when all the other leaves began to fall. Autumn turned to winter and still, Freddie held on, now shivering and all alone. Being a beautiful yellow leaf on a tall maple tree had lost its luster. Without warning, a gust of wind shook the tree and, before he knew it, he was falling, ever so gently to the ground to join the others. In time, he would realize that, in the cycle of life, it was not the end of his journey, but the beginning.

It's as Jesus told his disciples, "... unless a grain of wheat falls into the earth and dies, it remains alone; but if it dies, it bears much fruit." (*John 12:24 RSV*).

This mortal body is only a shell. It's not meant to last forever. That's the first point. The second is this: When you die, it doesn't matter if your body is embalmed, cremated, placed in a pine box and buried, or buried at sea. For that matter, it doesn't if your body is burned beyond recognition or blown to bits by an explosion. It's not this body that will be resurrected, but a glorified body. As Paul said, "... flesh and blood cannot inherit the kingdom of God." (*1 Corinthians 15:50 NIV*)

A question that's often asked is will we be able to recognize friends and loved ones in heaven? If so, at what age and stage of life will they be? Will a child who died in infancy forever remain a child? Will grandparents always be old?

If you read the obituaries, you've probably noticed how often the picture of the deceased doesn't match the write-up: A 90-something-year-old-man who died in the nursing home is pictured as a snappy young recruit in his military uniform; an elderly woman is pictured as a pert and pretty debutante. Why not? Don't you want to be remembered at your best?

So, we wonder: How will we be known in heaven? How will we be able to recognize those who've gone before us? The answer is: it's our glorified bodies by which we'll be known, bodies not defined by age or race or gender or anything else.

How do you envision that? I like to think of an infinite number of people clothed in their glorified bodies living in community with God and each other, yet knowing each other perfectly without blemishes, impediments, or faults. As Paul told the Corinthians:

"For now, we see only a reflection as in a mirror; then we shall see face to face. Now I know in part; then I shall know fully, even as I am fully known." (*1 Corinthians 13:12 NIV*).

It's a mystery in other words. As Paul told the Romans:

"I consider that the sufferings of this present time are not worth comparing with the glory that will be revealed to us, for the creation is eagerly waiting for the children of God to be revealed ... and not only the creation ... but we, who have the first fruits of the Spirit. We also groan inwardly as we eagerly wait for our adoption, the redemption of our bodies" (*Romans 8:18, 23 NIV*).

There was this couple living in Odessa, Texas years ago. The man's wife was in the latter stages of cancer, and he was trying to keep a stiff upper lip. They got to the stage where she signed up for hospice, and they set up a hospital bed for her in the living room where she wouldn't feel cooped up in the back of the house.

When it got close to the end, he called the kids and told them they'd better come right away. They got there the next day and took turns saying their goodbyes to their mother. He sat by her bedside off and on throughout the day. He'd hold her hand and, in her waking moments, they'd reminisce about the years they'd shared together. Toward evening, he read several passages of scripture to her: "The Lord is my shepherd, I shall not want ..." (*Psalm 23:1 RSV*); "Let not your hearts be troubled ... in my Father's house are many rooms ..." (*John 14-2 RSV*), "... (nothing) shall be able to separate us from the love of God in Christ Jesus our Lord..." (*Romans 8 NIV*). Then he turned to the 31st chapter of Proverbs, which begins:

"A good wife, who can find? She is far more precious than jewels. The heart of her husband trusts in her, and he will have no lack of gain." (*Proverbs 31:10-12 (RSV)*)

He read on until he got toward the end where it says,

"Her children rise up and call her blessed; her husband also, and he praises her (saying): 'Many women have done excellently, but you surpass them all.'" (*Proverbs 31:28-29 RSV*)

As he said the final words, she sighed and never took another breath. He said, "I knew she was gone, and I just sat there. Then I had the most unusual sensation. It was as if her soul just up and left her body … as if Jesus himself came down out of heaven and took her by the hand and led her home." He said, "To this day I still feel her presence. I see her smile and hear her laughter and know that she is with me, and I believe with all my heart that, one day, I'll see her again."

Brothers and sisters: You have a glorified body waiting for you. So do I, and so do all those who confess faith in Jesus Christ. He bought and paid for it with his own body and blood. He did it for you, so that, one day, you'll be clothed in this glorified body to live among the saints on high for all eternity. Let us pray:

Eternal God, give us grace to embrace this gift of mortal life, fleeting as it may be, as we claim the promise of eternal life through faith in Jesus Christ. Help us to live each day in faith, hope, and love, as we await the day when our bodies will be redeemed, and we will be united with all the saints in the glory of your heavenly kingdom. Amen

Epilogue

What follows is a story I wrote in 1984. Since it doesn't fit with the preacher stories in Part One or the sermons in Part Two, I've included it as a gift to you. In doing so I trust you will enjoy it, and I pray that it will serve you well when your cup is running dry, and you need a little "prime for the pump" to inspire your thoughts and restore your creative juices. Just remember when your cup is once again running over to think of others whose cups are running dry and leave enough prime for the pump to give them get a fresh start. ~ *Phil*

The Rainmaker

By Philip W. McLarty

Once upon a time there lived an eccentric old man by the name of Alexander Hydropolis. To be honest, Alexander wasn't that old but, dressed in tattered overalls and easily recognizable by his unruly long hair and beard, he always seemed older and wiser than his years. Because he seemed older and wiser, others often sought him out for his opinions on matters such as philosophy, engineering, folklore, and theology. Curious young boys, before their minds turned to girls, would often sit on the bench in front of Alexander's workshop and listen spellbound as he theorized about such things as the creation of the universe and the possibilities of perpetual motion.

Alexander lived in the little village of Hydropolis, named after his father, Aristotle, a Greek immigrant. As the story goes, Aristotle came to the New World in the 19th Century as an orphan, worked as cook's helper aboard ship to pay his passage, was taken in by a frontier family in Delaware on their westward trek, and struck out on his own when, in Southern Missouri, they crossed a mountain ridge overlooking a peaceful valley graced by a meandering stream. To the eyes of this 13-year-old boy the sight was heavenly. Declaring his independence, Aristotle gathered up his meager belongings, said goodbye to his host family, and set up camp beside the stream which he duly christened, "Ποταμός της Ζωής," a name in his native tongue meaning, "River of Life."

Aristotle wasted no time turning his campsite into a homestead and the surrounding area into a peaceful valley. Planning ahead, he built a dam upstream to control the water level, devised a system of irrigation, and laid out the plan of a city, complete with streets and parks and a town square at its center. To no one's surprise, he named the city after himself, Hydropolis. He then proceeded to find a wife and raise a family. Alexander was the first of five children to make Hydropolis his home. From the start, Alexander followed in his father's footsteps, always exploring, tinkering, and inventing new gadgets. Naturally, it was to Alexander that the townspeople turned in the wake of the great drought of 1923.

The rains stopped without warning in the summer of '22. No one saw it coming. Why, it was November before anyone paid any attention to how dry it was getting. Most just shrugged their shoulders and went about preparing for Thanksgiving. But when Christmas rolled around and it still had not rained, the mood shifted. Families sitting at tables of turkey and dressing and pumpkin pie could talk of little else. There was no cause for panic, but by late January the fields would need to be plowed and, if it hadn't rained by the end of February when the crops were planted, they'd be in serious trouble.

Sure enough, when all the ladies got together to plan the annual Valentine's Ball, their spirits were dampened by the lack of rain. The situation was tense. Emotions were fragile. Tempers flared over the least little things. Preachers prayed for rain, but with the prevailing winds being out of the east, no one really figured it would do any good. And it didn't.

So, it came as no surprise when, after church one day in late February, a group of men got together and paid a call on Mr. Hydropolis. They found him in his workshop sitting close to a wood burning stove whittling a dowel to replace one that had broken on an old kitchen chair. The men got right to the point. "We need rain, Mr. Hydropolis," they said, "and we need it bad." Alexander studied their faces and replied, "What does this have to do with me?" One of the men took the lead and said, "Begging your pardon, sir, but we figure if anyone can make it rain, you can. Will you at least give it a try?" Not normally a man given over to emotions, Alexander was moved by the men's desperation. "I'll give it some thought," he said. And that's all he had to offer.

Three weeks went by and still, no word from Mr. Hydropolis. By this time, the little village was near panic-stricken. The little River of Life had slowed to a trickle. Worse, the reservoir behind the dam was so low you could wade across it. To make the best of a bad situation, the men went to work on the dam dreaming of the day when it would, once again, be needed.

On Tuesday afternoon, the third week of March, 1923, completely without fanfare, Alexander opened the double doors in the back of his shop, cranked up his old Case tractor and pulled an odd-shaped piece of machinery out to the field behind. Mounted on a low-slung trailer, the contraption resembled a vintage fire engine with a pot-bellied boiler in the middle. Around the boiler were numerous valves and gauges and a large belt mechanism connecting the steam driven motor to what looked like a pump or fan. Once outside, Alexander erected a smokestack towering no less than thirty feet in the air.

Word spread quickly. It was clear that old man Hydropolis was up to something. In no time, a crowd gathered in the field behind his workshop. Whistling through his teeth, Alexander fired up the boiler and adjusted the valves. The big pump puffed a shaft of vapor into the air. The people looked on in astonishment. No one said a word. Finally, a little girl figured out what was going on and exclaimed, "He's gonna make it rain, Ma, he's gonna make it rain!" By this time the vapor had formed a small cloud. Still, the pump churned. In less than two hours the sky over the valley of Hydropolis was dark, the atmosphere laden with moisture.

The first drops of rain began to fall just before dark. By now, the whole community was on hand to celebrate. And what a celebration it was! Hats went flying. Voices rang out. Little children began to dance and sing, as older people bowed their heads and prayed. No one sought shelter, and no one went home. They just stood there getting drenched as the parched earth beneath their feet soaked up the refreshing rain.

It rained for the better part of three days before Alexander shut down the pump and closed off the valves. He fully intended to disassemble the apparatus and use the parts for something else, but no sooner than he started unbolting the smokestack, a group of men showed up. One spoke up, "Before you take that thing apart, Mr. Hydropolis, we were thinking how nice it would be to have such a machine standing by in case we need more rain to get the crops up." Alexander thought they might be on to something, so he said, "I don't see what it would hurt to let it sit for a while." Then, mulling over the thought at greater length, he went on to say, "As far as I'm concerned, I'll leave it here for as long as you like. That way, you can have rain anytime you want it."

The notion hit the men in a way they had not expected: Rain on demand? Imagine the possibilities! For now, the rainmaker stayed in the field, and the men went on their merry way.

By the end of the next week, they were back. "We were just thinking that it's about time for another shower," one said. "Do you think you might oblige us a couple of inches?" Alexander nodded and proceeded to fire up the boiler. In a few hours, rain began to fall. Simple as that. The pattern continued for several weeks – two or three men would hit up old man Hydropolis for more rain, and he would crank up the rainmaker and let it run until they'd had enough. Some said it was too good to be true, and perhaps it was. Others said it was the handiwork of the devil, tampering with the weather and such, and perhaps it was that as well. In time, the townspeople began to quarrel among themselves. Some said they needed yet more rain, others said they'd had enough. Some were angry because their plans were disrupted by the unexpected showers. Others countered, pointing out that rain is unpredictable by nature and has nothing to do with whether it comes about naturally or is man-made.

A lawyer posed a legal question, asking whether it was lawful to create a flow of water across another person's property, albeit by rain, without his consent. The clergy raised a theological objection contending that only God has the power to make it rain and the wisdom to determine when and where and how much. While it was unlike Mr. Hydropolis to debate any topic, he asked the Reverend

Mr. Hawthorne, "Do you not pray for the sick to get well and yet encourage them to consult a physician? Why should you not pray for rain and give the good Lord a little boost?" The question fell on deaf ears and was dismissed without comment.

The town council called an open meeting for the following Wednesday to let the people air their grievances and resolve their differences peacefully. Mr. Hydropolis hauled the rainmaker down to the town square to satisfy the more irrational minded that it was, after all, a harmless piece of machinery. The meeting was set for 2:00 p.m. in Town Hall, yet, by noon, the room was filled to overflowing. The mayor had hoped for an orderly meeting with a balanced discussion of the pros and cons. Such was not to happen. No sooner than the gavel sounded and the first speaker was called on to speak, the dialogue turned into a shouting match. By late afternoon, the townspeople were fully engaged in name calling and rehearsing old grievances many had hoped were long forgotten.

Mr. O'Leary, the mild-mannered blacksmith, was the first to leave. He told those standing by the back door, "It's turned into a donnybrook in there, it has," and quietly left the room. The men gave it little thought. Nor did they give it a second thought when, thirty minutes later, Mr. Hydropolis slipped out into the night. If they had been paying attention, they would have seen him walk over to the rainmaker and remove the control knobs and throw them as far as he could in different directions. Because there was so much bickering going on inside, they were looking the other way. In the meantime, Mr. Hydropolis fired up the boiler, set the machine in motion, and quietly walked away. He not only walked out of town, he walked across the valley and disappeared beyond the distant hills, never to be seen or heard of again.

Out of nowhere, a bolt of lightning lit the sky, and the thunder shook Town Hall. A heavy downpour soon followed. Someone looked out the front door and shouted, "The rainmaker, it's running full steam!" Several men rushed out into the storm to turn it off only to find the control knobs missing and the valves cranked wide open.

The next two hours passed at breakneck speed as the men

feverishly tried to shut down the rainmaker, yet all the forces were against them. The door to the firebox was jammed. No one had the necessary tools to open it. The night was pitch dark. The rain was unrelenting. They would have taken a different tack if they had only known how vulnerable they were. They would have left the rainmaker and fled to the hills. What they didn't know was that the reservoir was already at full capacity, due to the rains they had enjoyed over the past weeks. Despite their attempts to shore up the dam, the heavy downpour was more than it could stand. The townspeople were caught off-guard.

The dam broke at precisely 2:00 a.m. The waters swept across the little village of Hydropolis sparing no one. By sunrise the little river of life was safely back in its banks, and the only thing left of Hydropolis were the memories. What few survived soon moved on. The town was never rebuilt.

Years later, piecing together the all but forgotten history of her birthplace, a young mother returned to the town site with her seven-year-old son and told him the story of the great flood. When she finished, she sighed with regret, "I suppose you could say it was destined to happen. The tragedy of our ill-fated community was right there before us hiding in plain sight. If only we had had had eyes to see the connection: Hydropolis, "City of Water.""

Commentary

The promise of the gospel can be stated as simply as this: "Your heavenly father knows what you need before you ask him." (*Matthew 6:8 RSV*)

God knows we need rain. God knows we need food and clothing and shelter and loving relationships. God knows we need strong bodies and clear minds to function effectively and do his will. God knows all these things, but God is not a capricious being, causing it to rain here and not there, intentionally blessing some while withholding his blessings from others. Rather, God is a sovereign God, caring for the needs of all creation according to his will, being attentive to the cries of all his children regardless of whether they deserve it.

We deny faith in the steadfast love of God when we seek preferential treatment. Ironically, God shows his mercy by *not* acting according to our wishes. Think of the consequences if he did. What if we could determine when and where it would rain? Is the weather a dominion over which we would really like to be in control? What if we had the power to intervene in the natural processes of aging? Would anyone dare to be so bold as to turn back the clock?

We deny the sufficiency of God's grace when we seek to realign the creation to conform to our own wants and wishes. On the other hand, we open ourselves to the gifts of God's grace when we exercise patience and restraint, accepting the realities of life as they come, living in faith, and entrusting ourselves to God's benevolence. Take this home with you: Only as you let go of trying to order life to your own specifications will you be free to accept each new day as a gift of God filled with blessings from on high.

Meet the Author

Photo credit: *rodneysteelestudio@gmail.com*

Philip W. McLarty retired from pastoral ministry after more than fifty years in United Methodist and Presbyterian churches. He is the author of *The Children, Yes!* and *Seasons of the Christian Family,* (Discipleship Resources, Nashville). He is married to the former Kathleen Kavanagh Schooley of Hope, Arkansas, his hometown. He can be reached at *pwmclarty46@gmail.com.* Questions and comments are welcomed.

Printed in the United States
by Baker & Taylor Publisher Services